The Credit & Collection Manual

A Guide for Small Business

A publication of the
CREDIT RESEARCH FOUNDATION™

i

The Credit & Collection Manual
A Guide for Small Business

Credit Research Foundation™

Credit Research Foundation™
Columbia, Maryland 21045
410-740-5499

Printed in the United States of America

Copyright © 2002

By the Credit Research Foundation, Inc.

ISBN 0-939050-98-6

CONTENTS

FOREWORD

A firm's accounts receivable portfolio is often the largest asset on its balance sheet and, therefore, should be regarded in much the same way as any other commitment of corporate resources. Management must give the same attention to this capital investment as it does to manufacturing and distribution. Many owners of small businesses, though, often begin handling the credit function themselves, along with the other activities of purchasing, selling, financial planning and general office management. As their businesses grow, they find it increasingly difficult to give proper attention to the function of receivables management.

This handbook focuses on the role of credit in business and is geared towards *Small Businesses and Entrepreneurs*. It describes the qualifications and duties of the role of receivables management; explains the working tools that are available to the person performing the credit and collection tasks, discusses the objectives and needs of the credit function, and pinpoints certain measures for evaluating the receivables portfolio. It also describes the factors used to evaluate a customer, the means used to control exposure on accounts, and collection procedures that are basic to the job.

While discussing the fundamentals of these significant areas, this handbook is in no way intended to be a comprehensive manual; therefore, it necessarily abbreviates much of the theoretical background upon which the Credit profession is based. To further assist you, recognizing the time constraints placed upon you by the demands of day-to-day business activities, we have included a summary of key points at the end of each chapter. For a more detailed discussion of these issues, other publications from the Credit Research Foundation are available by subject matter.

CRF would like to thank a number of individuals who worked to bring this handbook to fruition. They include the project team that consisted of Sherry Mott of MeadWestvaco, David Needle of Pyramid Group, Richard Kulik of Sherwin Williams Co. and Rob Olsen of GE Capital Financial.

The foundation would also like to thank Jessica Butler of Grant Thornton, LLP for her advice, technical input and support, Andrea Clague and Terri Simms for their editorial assistance with this publication and Fred Hviid for his design work in the creation of the cover.

Lyle Paul Wallis, CCE   Terry Callahan, CCE
Executive Editor   President

ORGANIZING A CREDIT DEPARTMENT

Do I need a credit department?

Starting and maintaining a receivables management function can be quite a burden to a small business already faced with numerous issues and decisions. Although familiar with selling on credit, managing the resulting receivable and even the decision as to whether your customer is a good credit risk may not be as obvious. You may not have considered the need for a formal credit strategy or organized a separate credit function, as is usually found in larger businesses.

Like starting a business, developing a credit and collection function requires planning, execution of the plan, evaluating the results achieved and making corrections and modifications to the plan as required. To be most effective, plans and decisions that are made to establish a credit function, including your credit policy, collection practices, and the proper staffing arrangements should be consistent with the general objectives of your business. Additionally, as your business evolves and undergoes change, it is necessary to periodically review and revise your decisions and plans.

Even if you think your business is too small to justify a formal credit and collection department with people dedicated exclusively to the function, you should have a formal credit policy and documented collection practices to provide a consistent framework for decision making in the areas of credit and collection.

(Note: Appendix A at the end of this publication provides you with a guide for developing a Credit Strategy.)

What are the objectives of the credit & collection function?

The role of receivable management is more than just a guardian and protector of your investment in accounts receivable. The goal of receivables management is to achieve the best combination of profitable sales and timely collection of receivables (also known as accounts receivable turnover). These two elements will help to ensure a healthy return on the capital invested in your business. Since few businesses can be successful if they are not paid for the goods or services they deliver on credit; prudent credit and collection management can play an important role in contributing to the success of the business. The key objectives of intelligent credit management can be summarized as follows:

➢ Develop sound and constructive credit policies and practices that are consistent with the way you want to do business.

➢ Provide for prompt collection and adequate protection of your company's investment in accounts receivable (that means collect your money on time and try not to sell to those who cannot pay).

➢ Try to make sure that all credit decisions and actions will help to increase sales volume, add to customer stability and contribute to profits.

The importance of these objectives should not be underestimated. No business, large or small, can be effectively managed or achieve the best financial results possible without embracing these guidelines and striving to achieve the best results.

What is a credit policy?

While often broad in scope, policies lay the foundation upon which plans are formulated and decisions are made to reach the goals set by your organization's business plan and objectives.

A credit policy is intended to cover most of the credit decisions that need to be made by your company over an extended period of time. Answering the following six questions can provide the basic framework of your credit policy:

➢ What is your "mission statement" as it relates to credit? (e.g., how strict or lenient will you be when giving credit)

➢ What are your goals in terms of credit and receivables management? (e.g., bad debt, age of receivables, days sales outstanding, deductions)

➢ Who has responsibility for credit decisions?

➢ How is credit evaluated?

➢ How are collections handled?

➢ What are your terms of sale?

When formulating your credit policy and answering the questions outlined above, the following elements should be taken into consideration:

➢ Nature and size of your business

➢ Company objectives

➢ Product or service requirements

➢ Different classes or groups of customers

➢ Competitive conditions, market share

➢ Current business conditions, economic climate

➢ Profit margins

3

(Note: Appendix B at the end of this publication provides step-by-step guidance in answering these questions and developing a credit policy.)

While credit policies may be written or unwritten, we suggest a written policy, whenever possible, to ensure a common understanding among company personnel.

Why do companies have different credit policies?

Credit policies can vary greatly from company to company because they are largely dictated by the objectives of an individual business. There are no right or wrong answers when developing a credit policy, but your policy should reflect what is best for your firm. The level of risk your company is willing to accept when evaluating credit worthiness and the aggressiveness with which you pursue collections are two areas where companies can have wide variations. For example, a company that is striving to gain market share might be willing to accept more risk when evaluating the credit worthiness of a new customer than a company with a strong market position who is more concerned with cash flow. The table and discussion below outline four possible variations when looking at Credit Risk and Collection Efforts:

<table>
<tr><td colspan="2" rowspan="2"></td><td colspan="2">Collection Effort</td></tr>
<tr><td>Aggressive</td><td>Liberal</td></tr>
<tr><td rowspan="2">Credit Risk</td><td>Low</td><td>Low Risk
Aggressive Collections</td><td>Low Risk
Liberal Collections</td></tr>
<tr><td>High</td><td>High Risk
Aggressive Collections</td><td>High Risk
Liberal Collections</td></tr>
</table>

Low Credit Risk & Aggressive Collections: Under this policy, only high credit-rated accounts are accepted and very little variation from terms is allowed. The up-front analysis in determining the credit worthiness of your customer is thorough, and selling on credit may be denied to those customers who don't meet high credit standards. Collection efforts are vigorous and require a good deal of effort. This approach and the increased effort may pay sizable dividends in the form of improved accounts receivable turnover and minimal bad-debt losses lending to increased cash flow and profitability. However sales may be turned away by the unwillingness to take credit risks.

Low Credit Risk & Liberal Collections: This policy is somewhat more relaxed in its collection procedures. It concentrates on the selection of good credit risks, but does not aggressively press for payment. The assumption is that the good risks will, on average, pay their bills within terms; and if it takes them a little more time to pay, it is less expensive than the cost of following up with accounts that are only a few days past due. If your cost of capital is high (i.e., it costs you a lot to borrow money), this type of collection policy may not be wise since you need your money as soon as possible to minimize your borrowing requirements. In this situation, a more practical course might be to follow collections more closely.

High Credit Risk & Aggressive Collections: By emphasizing collections, this policy is the opposite of the one above. You are willing to assume a high credit risk, so the credit analysis is minimal, and nearly all customers that apply will be accepted. However, once the sale is made, close control is kept over collections. This type of policy would normally be followed in organizations selling high markup, low unit price goods or services or an organization trying to rapidly increase its market share. The cost of credit analysis is relatively low with this type of credit policy, but cost of the aggressive collection efforts can be quite high.

High Credit Risk & Liberal Collections: Very few businesses would find this type of credit policy profitable to operate. While it tends to have lower credit costs, the costs related to carrying receivables for long periods coupled with a resulting increase in bad debt expense due to high credit risk more than offsets the savings. The principal motivation for a company adopting this policy is to obtain maximum sales volume. For this policy to be effective, profit margins must be set high enough to counter the slow turn in receivables and resulting bad-debt losses.

Careful consideration of the advantages and disadvantages of each type of policy should help in choosing a good working credit policy for your particular business. Any policy must be somewhat flexible; but a firm, businesslike attitude should be maintained in the relationships with both the sales organization and customers. The terms of sale should be sound, practical, competitive and clearly expressed; the credit period should be clearly stated and adhered to as closely as possible.

What is the role of a receivables manager?

The receivables management function is responsible for approving credit and executing efficient collection practices in accordance with your company's credit policy. Prudent control and good judgment should be exercised to improve the sales potential of your company while protecting the collectibility of its accounts receivables. In the pursuit of this, it should be recognized that some bad-debt losses are to be expected and acceptable.

On an operating level, the responsibilities include gathering and maintaining up-to-date credit and financial information on your customers. The information collected and retained should serve as the basis for a decision on an individual order or on an account as a whole. The credit investigation should be conducted with the view of finding reasons to approve, not disapprove credit. Informed decisions should be based upon current economic conditions, both nationally and locally. Assuming the account is desirable from a product distribution point of view, a receivables manager must determine a customer's willingness and ability to pay. *(Chapter IV discusses the credit investigation in further detail.)*

Functional responsibility also includes the collection of accounts receivable. Once a sale has been made, you must work to ensure the timely collection of monies due. This often requires a good working relationship with your customer. If practical, you should visit with key customers to promote favorable customer-credit-sales relations. *(Chapter VI discusses specific collection procedures in further detail.)*

If you have (or are looking to create) a distinct receivables manager position, whom this person reports to is important. Since the focus of the sales department is on increasing sales and the focus of credit is to make prudent credit decisions, frequently there is a natural tendency for sales and credit to find themselves on opposite sides of a credit discussion. Therefore, to achieve the balance necessary between credit and sales policies, the credit function generally reports to a key financial executive.

As part of the management team, the receivables manager should participate in the development of credit policy, be empowered with the authority to implement the policy, and be tasked with carrying out the credit and collection activities.

If you are looking to hire a receivables manager, it is important to first write out a job description defining the desired qualifications and characteristics. A college graduate who has majored in business administration and understands the principles of accounting and credit should, with experience, make a good credit professional. On the other hand, an individual who has already gained sound knowledge of business and financial practices through experience (rather than education) and is determined to make a contribution to the success of the enterprise would also make a good candidate. Good judgment, tact and initiative in carrying out the credit function are all attributes of a successful credit manager.

6

Moreover, the more familiar the credit manager is with all phases of the business, the more effectively they can do their job. These include the problems of the production department in forecasting and scheduling output, knowledge of company sales policy, familiarity with the marketing characteristics peculiar to each product being distributed, and understanding the operation of each customer's business.

The following character traits are frequently associated with the successful credit professional:

➢ Shows initiative and drive, a self-starter
➢ Adaptable and resourceful in meeting new situations and changing conditions
➢ Able to handle customer and internal relations diplomatically and firmly when required
➢ Able to communicate effectively and convincingly both verbally and in writing
➢ Analytical and detail-oriented
➢ Able to measure risk and analyze problems thoroughly and constructively
➢ Willingness to take considered risks for profitable company growth
➢ Perseveres when handling difficult situations
➢ Creative in eliciting information
➢ Fairness and reasonableness in dealing with people
➢ Able to absorb and retain details
➢ Open attitude toward change, particularly in systems and procedures

(Note: Appendix C at the end of this publication provides guidance on developing a job description.)

ORGANIZING A CREDIT DEPARTMENT
Chapter Summary

This Chapter Answers the Following Questions:

➢ Do I need a credit department?

➢ What are the objectives of a credit & collection department?

➢ What is a credit policy?

➢ Why do companies have different credit policies?

➢ What is the role of a receivables manager?

Key Points

➢ Many small businesses underestimate the importance of having a formal, documented credit policy.

➢ The goal of credit management is to achieve the best combination of profitable sales and timely collection of accounts receivable.

➢ A credit policy should cover most of the credit decisions that need to be made by a company over an extended period of time and should answer the following questions:

- What is your "mission statement" as it relates to credit?

- What are your goals in terms of credit and receivables management?

- Who has responsibility for credit decisions?

- How is credit evaluated?

- How are collections handled?

- What are your terms of sale?

➢ Credit policies can vary greatly from company to company. The level of risk a company is willing to accept when evaluating credit worthiness and the aggressiveness with which they pursue collections are dictated by the objectives of an individual business.

➢ Responsibilities in the management of receivables include:

- Gathering and maintaining current credit and financial information on the company's customer base.

- Making decisions as to the credit worthiness of potential and existing customers.

- Ensuring the timely collection of accounts receivable.

Knowledge is free...
Get all you can.
www.crfonline.org

Visit the Credit Assistant at the
Credit Research Foundation's website.

MAINTENANCE OF CREDIT FILES AND RECORDS

In receivables management you must have certain working tools to maintain the expected degree of efficiency. One such tool, the customer credit files and their contents, is of prime importance to good credit management. All information files should be kept in a permanent file section at hand for ready reference whether electronic or manual. The material in it should be retained as long as it remains useful in rendering a credit decision.

What is a customer credit file?

A credit file is established to store all the gathered data. It is an accumulation of credit information in whatever form available. The efficiency of the file depends upon its content and the speed with which it may be analyzed and used.

Credit information must be gathered promptly and efficiently while being mindful of the element of cost. It may be generated internally, or in the case of a new account, obtained from outside sources. Information derived from previous experience with a customer includes knowledge about the principals, an understanding of how the business operates, and information on the customer's purchasing and paying habits. On a new account, more reliance is placed on outside sources, such as the bank, other suppliers and reporting agencies.

A credit file should normally include analysis of financial data, banking arrangements, trade payments, necessary agreements and other relevant information. These records should be maintained in a uniform manner to permit ready comparison and evaluation over a period of time.

Documents and collateral obtained to secure a credit appraisal are stored separately, usually in a fireproof cabinet or vault.

Collection correspondence is usually kept in a special follow-up file, but unless it contains something noteworthy it can be destroyed after collection is completed. The credit file, be it manual or automated, should not be cluttered with outdated information, unless the information has value as a basis for future credit consideration. Whenever a loss is incurred, the complete file information should be retained indefinitely, available for inspection by financial management or, outside auditors.

Credit Instructions. When a credit decision has been made, the record of that decision takes the form of credit instructions placed in the credit file. In their simplest form, instructions merely state a customer's name and address, the credit line, terms of sale, and billing instructions. These items can be briefly noted in the credit file. This procedure is commonly used when the credit department handles a large volume of small accounts with relatively few special problems.

If credit checking on each individual order is unnecessary, instructions should be plainly marked "No Credit Review," to avoid duplication of effort. If it is the practice to dispense with credit lines completely on accounts where no credit check is considered necessary, the instructions should be marked "Requirements." Either of the above designations will reduce credit-checking requirements to a minimum.

In the case where orders are being processed by an automated system, the system should be configured to pass through orders that don't require further scrutiny and flag orders on customers whose accounts have fallen into a delinquent status or those that need further review by credit.

More elaborate credit instructions may be needed in some instances to cover advanced dating for seasonal shipments, to specify cash discount privileges, and to provide for multiple credit lines for the same customer. The instructions may also indicate the amount and kind of collateral that will be accepted for secured amounts, and release arrangements for collateral.

File Revision. It is of utmost importance to revise information on active accounts often enough to support your judgment and to watch for any change or trend. Stale information may be misleading and costly. To determine the status of an account the credit file must contain up-to-date information. A consistent method of revision must be followed, whether it is done on a regular or on an exception basis. Periodic purging of files will weed out obsolete material and keep the file manageable.

What is the role of automation in credit management?

Automation has become indispensable to credit operations. Because of a computer's ability to store data, it fulfills the credit department's needs to retain information on a customer's bill-paying performance and to monitor a customer's financial status. The use of automated systems to manage accounts on an exception basis highlights the importance of computers for credit tasks that are routine and can be programmed.

Selection of automated procedures for the credit function and accounts receivable operation are influenced by the following points:

➢ Objectives to be accomplished
➢ Information needed to accomplish these objectives
➢ Data necessary to provide the information
➢ Method of converting the data into such information

The automated system must provide you with the information necessary to control accounts receivable and to keep adequate records of experience with customers. Therefore, the system must be geared to:

➢ Establish customer accounts

➢ Record all transactions affecting those accounts

➢ Permit prompt notification of past-due balances with an adequate means for collection follow-up

➢ Provide some comprehensive record of past activity with each customer

All account information is stored on disks, tapes or imaged and can be retrieved in a variety of forms, e.g., paper printouts or on-screen displays. Most of these systems include such automated features as:

➢ Updating of customer history

➢ Credit approval or rejection based on predetermined credit lines and any delinquency situation

➢ Preparation of past-due statements and other collection reminders

➢ Preparation of unearned cash discount and other short-payment notices

Most receivables managers have learned to adapt their daily operations to automated methodologies. They have learned that when the systems have been properly planned and programmed, the data formerly available from paper files and the customer ledger card is now fully available through the automated system. Once automated, the receivables management process should be restructured to take full advantage of the efficiencies created from automation.

MAINTENANCE OF CREDIT FILES AND RECORDS

Chapter Summary

This Chapter Answers the Following Questions:

➢ What is a customer credit file?

➢ What is the role of automation in credit management?

Key Points:

➢ A credit file is established to store all the gathered data. It is an accumulation of credit information in whatever form available.

➢ A credit file should normally include analysis of financial data, banking arrangements, trade payments, necessary agreements and other relevant information.

➢ When a credit decision has been made, the record of that decision takes the form of credit instructions placed in the credit file. In their simplest form, instructions merely state the customer's name and address, the credit line, terms of sale, and billing instructions.

➢ It is important to revise information on active accounts often enough to support your judgment and to watch for any change or trend.

➢ The use of automated systems to manage accounts on an exception basis highlights the importance of computers for credit tasks that are routine and can be programmed.

➢ The system should be geared to:

- Establish customer accounts
- Record all transactions affecting those accounts
- Permit prompt notification of past-due balances with an adequate means for collection follow-up
- Provide some comprehensive record of past activity with each customer

➢ Automated features should include:

- Updating of customer history
- Credit approval or rejection based on predetermined credit lines and delinquency
- Preparation of past-due statements and other collection reminders
- Preparation of unearned cash discount and other short-payment notices

CREDIT DECISION-MAKING

The proper approach to credit decision-making should be to look for ways to approve orders, with a reasonable expectation that payment will be made in accordance with terms. All too often we see receivables managers looking for reasons to refuse orders without searching hard enough for reasons to approve. The more constructive approach is to try to approve profitable orders, recognizing the dangers and seeking whatever additional protection is available.

What do I consider in handling customer orders?

A decision to grant credit affects revenue, sales, profits, production and procurement. An approved order may take several forms:

➤ The order may be approved as submitted.

➤ The order may be approved for a smaller amount on the same trade terms.

➤ The order may be approved for the submitted amount on different terms.

➤ The order may be approved for a smaller amount on different terms.

Orders must be processed rapidly, if shipments are to be made promptly; and the system of credit checking should be geared for speed and efficiency. If the account is a good risk, the order may be approved as is. Otherwise, an alternative must be proposed to the sales people and the customer. It will be necessary, on occasion, to hold orders for payment of past-due bills or for additional investigation when all the essential facts are not available immediately. An effective order holding procedure is one that promptly notifies your customer of the reason and points toward a remedy lending to shipment of the order while maintaining good will. Usually, a telephone call or a diplomatic e-mail or form letter will serve the purpose. Of course, prompt release of such orders when your customer meets the requested conditions is a necessity for preserving customer good will.

How should I set credit lines?

As soon as possible after the first-order approval, controls should be established to ensure prompt and appropriate disposition of future orders. The basic means of control is the credit line, which indicates the maximum amount of risk to be taken on any customer.

Credit lines commonly serve as guides for order approval, minimize upward referral of orders and call immediate attention to any change in a customer's purchasing or paying habits. Any order that does not exceed the credit line can be approved without further investigation or analysis. An order exceeding the line signals the need for examination of the account at a higher level.

Your customer's credit line should be based on two major factors:

1. Requirements by your customer for your products.
2. The ability of your customer to pay its debts timely.

Other factors to consider include your company's policy and objectives, demand for your company's product, the size and financial condition of your company and the extent of your competition.

Lines of credit are based on assumptions, experiences, estimates and forecasts. Consequently, developments that affect the willingness or ability of a customer to pay should be the focus of the receivables manager.

A review of the account is required when:

➢ An order exceeds the credit line

➢ When a customer requests extraordinary amounts

➢ When the account falls into a delinquent status

➢ When customers request extended terms

➢ When some information concerning a particular customer is deemed significant

How should I classify my customer base?

While systems for credit investigation and credit approval vary from business to business, some of the elements involved are quite basic. The first step is to classify all accounts into good, fair or marginal credit risks.

Good Credit Risks. Accounts classified as *good* credit risks are those that are long established, soundly financed and well rated. They pose the fewest credit problems. Many can be included on a list for automated credit approval within certain predetermined dollar lines. Periodic review of these accounts is necessary in order to identify changes in status that might have occurred; but essentially, individual order checking is unnecessary.

Fair Credit Risks. Accounts classified as *fair* are those that are stable and ordinarily prompt or only slightly slow in making payment. These require a closer check and a more frequent review to avoid troublesome situations.

Marginal Credit Risks. Marginal accounts represent acceptable customers that require close attention, and it is on these accounts that the majority of time will be spent. They usually are ones with acceptable management and sales ability, but with operating capital limitations that might cause slow payments. Degrees of marginality exist; a business that may be considered marginal by one company might not be viewed as such by another. However, the standard for accepting credit business from this type of account should be determined and set forth in the selling company's credit policy.

What should trigger the review of a previous credit decision?

All customers should undergo periodic credit reviews. The exact time period for each customer review may vary but no customer should go longer than one year without a review of their credit and financial status. In addition, as business conditions and the circumstances of individual customers change, it frequently becomes necessary to review previous credit decisions, taking these changes into consideration. Company procedures should specify when a credit decision needs to be reviewed because of changes in payment experience, new financial statements or agency reports, and overall credit department experience with days sales outstanding (DSO - see page 58), past due accounts, and bad-debt losses.

What steps can be taken to minimize credit risk?

When a credit risk associated with a customer appears weak and unacceptable, your first choice would be to accept the order on a cash or prepaid basis. If this is not possible, rather than make a flat rejection, you may want to consider making special written arrangements with that customer in the form of a consignment or security agreement to ensure payment and avoid loss of the sale. Here, you are able to take measures under Article 9 of the Uniform Commercial Code to create a valid security interest in favor of your business on specified property. As a secured party you can protect your claim to property you sold against the claims of third parties, by filing a financing statement to perfect your interest in the property covered by a consignment or security agreement. In most cases, an attorney familiar with the working of the Uniform Commercial Code should be consulted before making such arrangements.

(Note: The CRF publication Secured Transactions will provide you greater detail on securing your customers indebtedness to you.)

What is credit insurance?

A credit insurance policy provides protection against disastrous bad-debt losses. It does not eliminate bad debt write-offs but allows you to hedge against catastrophic loss. It is not a substitute for competent credit analysis but does relieve some of the pressure on you to make an appropriate credit granting decision. A credit insurance policy protects against excessive bad-debt loss, promotes safe sales expansion, provides effective collection assistance, strengthens your borrowing and purchasing power and provides loss prevention guidance on key risks.

Credit Decision-Making

Chapter Summary

This Chapter Answers the Following Questions:
- What should I consider in handling customer orders?
- How should I set credit lines?
- How should I classify my customer base?
- What should trigger the review of a previous credit decision?
- What steps can be taken to minimize credit risk?
- What is credit insurance?

Key Points:
- The basic approach to credit decision-making should be to seek ways to approve orders, with a reasonable expectation that payment will be made in accordance with terms.
- A decision to grant credit affects revenue, sales, profits, production and procurement. The approved order may take several forms:
  - The order may be approved as submitted.
  - The order may be approved for a smaller amount on the same trade terms.
  - The order may be approved for the submitted amount on different terms.
  - The order may be approved for smaller amount on different terms.
- Orders must be processed rapidly; if shipments are to be made promptly, and the system of credit checking should be geared for speed and efficiency.
- As soon as possible after the first-order approval, controls should be established to ensure prompt and appropriate disposition of future orders. The basic means of control is the credit line, which indicates the maximum amount of risk to be taken on any customer.
- A customer's credit line should be based on two major factors:
  - Requirements by your customer for your products.
  - The ability of the customer to pay their debts timely.
- As business conditions and the circumstances of individual customers change you should schedule a review of previous credit decisions.
- When a credit risk associated with a customer appears weak and unacceptable, your first choice would be to accept the order on a cash or prepaid basis. If this is not possible, rather than make a flat rejection, you can consider a Consignment or Security Agreement.

17

CREDIT INVESTIGATION

How extensive should my credit investigation be?

Essentially, a credit investigation is the gathering of pertinent facts. Since response time is often a vital factor, decisions must be made promptly, and determining how much information is needed for a sound decision is important. The extent of the credit investigation varies with each case. When deciding how extensive an investigation to make, the following points should be considered:

➢ Size of order received

➢ Potential of the customer for future orders

➢ Status of the customer and length of time in business

➢ Risk in relation to margin of profit on sale

➢ Nature of the product sold, (i.e. seasonal or staple)

➢ Competitive nature of the sale

➢ Class of customer being sold

➢ Time available prior to the specified delivery date

➢ Total credit exposure of the customer

➢ Dictates of your credit policy

 Particular caution in credit appraisals is advisable on orders of a special nature that require processing or fabrication to the specifications of the buyer. Ordinarily, once such merchandise has been prepared, it is not marketable to other customers.

What are the C's of credit?

The entire credit system is based on confidence and good judgment. Therefore, an investigation is conducted to determine if a customer is acting in good faith and is not overestimating its future ability to pay. The two questions uppermost in the credit manager's mind are:

➢ Can the customer pay?

➢ Will the customer pay?

Credit worth is determined by careful consideration of certain basic factors sometimes referred to as the C's of credit: character, capacity, capital and conditions of the times.

Character. This includes the willingness of the debtor to pay obligations. To properly develop an idea of the business character of an organization and its management, you must know as much as possible about the customers previous business habits and the business history of its management.

For a customer who's management has been in business previously, or who has been a member of the management staff of another business, information concerning their character while in that capacity should be assessed. This information should reflect the record of their success, the capacities in which they were employed and how they performed.

For potential customers who have set up a business for the first time, caution should be exercised in the judgment of their ability, conscientiousness, integrity and aggressiveness. A personal visit is often warranted to help determine that the *new in business entrepreneur* meets the specific traits essential for business survival.

Capacity. This deals with the ability of your customer to operate successfully, thereby ensuring that they will continue in business and be able to pay their bills. A business may be regarded as an operation of three separate, specialized, and interlocking functions: marketing, production or service, and finance. To be successful, the principals must successfully integrate each of these areas into the business. Otherwise, the lacking ingredient will limit successful operations.

In a very small business, one person frequently handles all three functions. As the business expands it often becomes necessary to split the functions and to assign them to knowledgeable people who will devote most of their time to them. If the principals cannot provide the specialized knowledge or abilities, those services must be purchased from the outside.

Previous business experience is again a valid indicator of the capacity of a firm. Particularly when large volume orders, exacting specifications or tight delivery schedules are involved, you should focus on identifying whether the concern appears to have the proper capacity in place.

Capital. In this phase, you should seek to determine whether the customer would be able to pay its obligations timely. This approach is different from that of the first "C," which seeks to judge if they will be willing to pay.

This element highlights the financial condition and trend of operations. Each case is judged on its own merits, since many factors affect the financial conditions of a business. In some lines of business, a large investment is needed in fixed assets. Others require only a minimum investment in machinery and fixtures. This affects the financial picture of the concern. Similarly, some lines of business must have large amounts of ready cash and liquid assets to meet seasonal operating expenses, while others can rely on regular cash flow to meet maturing debts.

You should strive to gain an understanding of your customer's liquidity position and assure that sufficient liquid assets or available open lines of bank credit exist to meet short-term obligations in a timely manner.

The trend of the business is significant and weighs heavily in the overall judgment of the account. You should look more favorably on a business that shows increasing sales, profits and net worth.

Conditions of the Times. General economic conditions in the nation, in the community, and in the industry will exert a modifying influence on the final analysis of the account. At any particular time, certain industries will be on the up-trend, while others will be stagnant or in a downward spiral. The likelihood of a satisfactory credit experience is greater when the subject is in an industry that is in a period of growth.

Likewise, during prosperous times, risk of credit loss is generally less than it is during a depressed period. Regional economic conditions also affect the likelihood that your customers will pay their bills on time, since they must rely upon receipts from their own customers. For example, a major plant closure within a specific community could have a significant impact on local merchants.

What are the principal sources of credit information?

Sound credit decisions can only be made on the basis of adequate information covering the nature of your customer's business, the character of the principals, its financial condition and other matters. If you have previously done business with an applicant, the information on hand must be brought up to date. If it is a new account; however, the job of collecting facts may become more difficult. The principal sources of credit information are as follows.

Sales Requests for Credit Information. Sales representatives, your company's first contact with a new customer and the most frequent contact with an established customer, are an excellent potential source of credit information. They should be trained to submit credit applications with all prospective accounts, new accounts or both. Credit applications vary considerably in their scope. Generally an effective credit application provides the business name and address, how the business is organized (corporation, partnership, or proprietorship), lines of business, method of operation and the length of time in business. Additionally, the application should provide bank and trade reference information. The application should spell out the your terms of sale and provide an acknowledgement section that your customer signs indicating that he has read and understands the selling terms and agrees to adhere to them. Most firms and individuals are conditioned to the necessity of furnishing credit and financial information to support credit transactions and generally the information requested on the credit application will be provided as a matter of course.

(Note: Appendix D at the end of this publication provides you with an example of a Credit Application.)

Each member of your sales department should understand company credit policy and know enough about credit to report pertinent information promptly. Credit policies and terms should be made known to customers when an order is taken. Such cooperation from the sales department not only increases the efficiency of the credit department in fulfilling its responsibility of creating more profitable sales but also helps speed collections and prevents misunderstandings.

Customer-Supplied Information. There is no better source of information about a business than from the business itself. Direct contact with the principals provides the credit manager with financial details, bank and trade references, and other information of importance. How this information is requested and obtained will depend upon the time available, the location of the customer, the relative importance of the credit exposure, and the degree of cooperation that can be obtained from your customer.

Direct contact enables you as a supplier to establish a close and friendly working relationship and build mutual confidence and respect. It provides you with an opportunity to gain an insight into the character of your customers' management and the capacity of that management to effectively implement necessary business operations. In addition to providing access to information, direct contact can be used to clarify terms of sale and clear the way for a continuing relationship with your customer.

Bank Information. Commercial banks provide a variety of services to fulfill the needs of their customers. They accept deposits and honor checks written against them, accept and pay drafts, execute wire transfers, issue letters of credit, provide safe deposit boxes for storage of valuables, and lend money. Most of their loans are of a short-term nature, though many banks also make term loans of three years and longer. The loans may be unsecured or secured by collateral.

Your bank can be an invaluable source of credit information. You can make your own inquiries of your customer's bank or you may ask your bank to inquire on your behalf. In either case, the information is helpful in obtaining a rounded picture of the customer's financial condition.

Information to be verified includes length of time as a bank customer, deposit balances (checking, saving, CD's, etc.), and lines of credit (amount of credit line, loan origination date, current availability of the line, expiration date, loan restrictions, and an understanding of loan covenants).

21

The information provided by the bank can serve as a good indicator of your customers' ability to pay. Covenant information is also very important. If your customer is in violation of one or more of the loan covenants the bank has the right to pull the line of credit. Even if the firm could finance its operations internally, without a bank line, it is very likely that its pay patterns would slow down.

Trade Information. This consists of information that is obtained from other merchandise suppliers of your customer. It can include such data as the recent high credit extended, amount owing, amount past due, whether customer payments are discounted, prompt or slow and, if slow, how many days; whether a supplier has referred the account to a collection agency, and other facts about the buying and paying record of your customer. This is vital information. It describes how your customer actually pays bills, regardless of other financial facts.

Your customer's payment record should be examined for specifics as well as for the trend of payments and be reconciled with the condition indicated by their financial statements. Though slow trade payments can be a signal of trouble, it may also characterize a business that is having growing pains but is substantially healthy; its slowness may be seasonal or due to expansion.

Trade information, like bank information, is an important part of the credit file. It should be complete or at least representative of your customer's payment record. A customer opening a new account should be asked for the names of its suppliers. You should also check with other likely suppliers, since references given by the customer usually will report a good paying record. The payment pattern with all suppliers is needed, including those that the customer may be paying slowly.

Depending upon your customer, the industry, location, size of order and other factors, you have several places to get this information. The most commonly used include the National Association of Credit Management, industry credit groups; credit reporting agencies, such as Dun & Bradstreet & Experian, and direct interchange with other suppliers.

Information that is readily available through credit reporting agencies and from industry credit groups reflect the character of the principles, history of the business, if the company is currently involved in litigation and how the firm meets its financial obligations. With this information in hand, you can often develop a mental picture of your customer and what it would be like to do business with them.

Credit Investigation

This Chapter Answers the Following Questions:
- ➤ How extensive should my credit investigation be?
- ➤ What are the C's of credit?
- ➤ What are the principal sources of credit information?

Key Points:
- ➤ The extent of a credit investigation varies with each case. Some points to consider in deciding how extensive an investigation should be include:
    - Size of order received
    - Potential of the customer for future orders
    - Status of customer and length of time in business
    - Risk in relation to margin of profit on sale
    - Nature of product sold, (i.e. seasonal or staple)
    - Competitive nature of the sale
    - Class of customer being sold
    - Time available prior to specified delivery date
    - Total credit exposure of customer
    - Dictates of your credit policy
- ➤ An investigation is conducted to determine if a customer is acting in good faith and is not overestimating its future ability to pay. The two questions uppermost in your mind are:
    - Can the customer pay?
    - Will the customer pay?
- ➤ Credit worth is determined by careful consideration of certain basic factors sometimes referred to as the C's of credit:.
    - Character
    - Capacity
    - Capital
    - Conditions of the times
- ➤ If you have previously done business with an applicant, the information on hand must be brought up to date. If it is a new account, the principal sources of credit information should include:
    - Sales requests for credit information

- Customer-supplied information
- Bank Information
- Trade Information

➢ Information that is readily available through credit reporting agencies and from industry credit groups reflect the character of the principles, history of the business, if the company is currently involved in litigation and how the firm meets its financial obligations.

FINANCIAL STATEMENT ANALYSIS

What is financial statement analysis?

A key component to the credit decision-making process is the financial analysis of a customer's financial condition. Such an analysis involves an examination of their balance sheet, income statement, statement of cash flows, supporting schedules, and consideration of economic conditions generally as well as in the customer's industry.

(Note: An Excel based Financial Analysis Model, that provides you with an automated tool to conduct customer financial analysis, may be obtained free of charge from CRF, by requesting it online at www.crfonline.org)

Analysis of a financial statement may be divided into two general categories: internal and comparative. Internal analysis uses figures from the financial statements of a given date or period to gain an understanding of the financial condition of the company. Comparative analysis may be used to determine trends when two or more successive sets of figures are reviewed, or may be used to evaluate a given company's financial statement against industry standards. These methods may be used separately or in combination and provide some of the basic information that enables you as an experienced receivables manager to reach a sound credit decision.

The discussion that follows outlines many important points that should be considered when financial statements are examined.

How do you determine the reliability of the financial data?

Before you begin your analysis of the financial statements, you should assess the reliability of the financial data. There are four basic types of financial statements: audited, reviewed, compiled and management prepared.

Audited Statements offer the most reliability. Audited Statements are prepared by a Certified Public Accountant and undergo a rigorous examination for their accuracy and compliance with Generally Accepted Accounting Principals (GAAP).

Reviewed Statements are prepared by the accountant from the books of the client. The accountant performs limited inquiry and analytical procedures. Limited assurance is given that the statements conform to GAAP.

Compiled Statements are also prepared by an outside accountant from the books and records of the client. The compilation does not include any review or verification of procedures. The accountant assumes no responsibility or liability for the financial information.

Management Prepared Statements are statements prepared in-house by an organization's management. There is no assurance that the information contained in these statements reflects an accurate accounting of the business' finances.

What is the Balance Sheet?

The Balance Sheet provides a snapshot picture of the financial condition of a company at a given point in time. It is a statement of assets, liabilities and net worth reflecting the company's financial position at the date indicated on the statement. Essential items include

Assets. These are resources owned by a company. They may take several forms, such as cash, accounts receivable, inventory or physical property. They may be fully paid, in which case they are held free and clear, or they might be owned subject to outstanding debt. In any case, title to the assets is in the company's name.

Liabilities. These are the amounts owed by a company. Current liabilities, by long-accepted definition, are obligations maturing (coming due) within one year from the date of the statement on which they appear. Also included are demand notes that, although carrying no maturity date, may be presented for payment any time at the option of the holder. Mortgages, bonds, debentures and long-term notes that mature more than one year from the statement date represent deferred or long-term liabilities. Included in this category are demand notes that have been formally subordinated to all other creditors for a period of at least one year from the date of the statement under consideration.

Net Worth. The equity of unincorporated business firms may be called net worth, proprietary interest, partners' capital or capital. Drawings and withdrawals of capital during the auditing period are reflected in the operating statement and the balance sheet.

Corporate net worth or stockholders' equity is divided into various classes of outstanding stock and retained earnings. The analyst should gain an understanding of any asset or dividend preferences involved in the classes of stocks, as well as in the relationship between owned and borrowed funds.

What is the Income Statement?

Also called the profit and loss statement, the income statement shows the results of a business operation over a given period of time. When issued for credit purposes, this statement may vary from a complete schedule to a severely condensed version of the audit report. A complete income statement shows sales, cost of goods sold, gross profit, expenses, net operating income, other income and expenses, federal income taxes, and net income.

What is the Statement of Changes in Financial Position?

The *Statement of Changes in Financial Position* is a statement that shows the cause of a change in working capital. This statement can be extremely useful for analyzing financial strength. It presents financial information in two separate parts. One, called sources and uses of funds, reports the flow of funds during the period among the various asset, liability, and net worth accounts. The other, called statement of cash flows, provides a further refinement in the examination of the flow of funds by measuring the changes taking place in the net working capital during the period under review.

What type of internal analysis should I perform?

Performing internal analysis helps you understand your customer. It calls for an examination of items within a single financial statement for judging their significance in relation to the capital of the company, its method of operation, and conditions prevailing within the industry. When sales, profits or other operating details are not available, emphasis must be placed on internal analysis of the balance sheet. The major tools for internal analysis are balance sheet ratios and a working knowledge of the line of business, including the method of operation and seasonal influences.

As an important first step in internal analysis, the financial statement should be examined for validity and general correctness. After this has been completed, ratios should be calculated. With ratios, it is possible to determine if asset and liability relationships are reasonably aligned. As ratios vary from industry to industry, it is difficult to provide a single benchmark to let you know whether a given ratio is "good or bad". As further discussed at the end of this chapter, two sources for industry benchmark ratios include Risk Management Association and Dun & Bradstreet.

Ratios focus on four areas:
- Liquidity
- Solvency
- Efficiency
- Profitability

27

The most important ratios are summarized as follows:

Liquidity Ratios - Can your customer pay you on time?

Liquidity ratios evaluate a company's ability to convert short-term assets into cash to cover their short-term obligations (debts). They are useful tools in determining the creditworthiness of your customer's account.

Working Capital. Working capital compares current assets to current liabilities and serves as the liquid reserve available to satisfy contingencies and uncertainties. A high working capital balance is mandated if the entity is unable to borrow on short notice. The ratio indicates the short term solvency of a business and helps in determining if a firm can pay its current liabilities when due.

Working Capital = Current Assets - Current Liabilities

Current Ratio. The current ratio measures the relationship between current assets and current liabilities and is determined by dividing the current assets by the current liabilities. Current assets are basically the sum of cash, short-term marketable securities, notes and accounts receivable, and merchandise inventories. Current debt is the total of all liabilities falling due within one year. Usually the higher the ratio, the greater the protection afforded the short-term creditor. It is generally conceded that cash and receivables have higher liquidating values than merchandise. Consequently, if cash and receivables are high in relation to inventory, a lower current ratio could be satisfactory from a credit standpoint.

Current Ratio = Current Assets
Current Liabilities

Quick Ratio. Also called the liquid ratio or acid test, the quick ratio is the ratio of the sum of cash, marketable securities and receivables to current liabilities. It should provide at least a small margin over current debts. A high quick ratio can often support a low current ratio. If the ratio is too low, a firm must rely on quick sale of merchandise for funds to meet maturing debts. A slow turnover of receivables worsens the quality of the quick ratio. Within this ratio, the ideal is to see the cash item equal to one month's expenses of the business.

Quick Ratio = Cash + Marketable Securities + Accounts Receivable
Current Liabilities

28

Solvency Ratios - What is the likelihood your customer will pay you at all?

Solvency ratios determine the degree of protection afforded suppliers of long-term funds and can aid in judging the firms ability to raise additional funds. These ratios demonstrate the firm's ability to make creditors whole in the event of bankruptcy or forced liquidation.

Total Debts to Assets. This computation provides information about a company's ability to handle reductions in assets arising from losses without jeopardizing the interest of creditors.

Total Debts to Assets = Total Liabilities
Total Assets

Debt to Equity. In this computation, the liabilities include all funded debt (long-term liabilities) as well as current debts. The ratio is broader than current debt to tangible net worth, since it includes the risk of long-term creditors. It is an indicator of the firm's ability to leverage, and of the relative investments made in the firm by stockholders and by all creditors. A high ratio indicates high leveraging and potential danger to creditors.

Debt to Equity = Total Debt
Total Equity

Interest Coverage Ratio. This computation is indicative of a company's capacity to meet interest payments. The formula incorporates EBIT (Earnings Before Interest and Taxes). The higher the ratio the more able the business is to cover interest costs and retain earnings. The ratio is particularly meaningful in the analysis of highly leveraged businesses.

Interest Coverage Ratio = EBIT
Interest Expense

Long-Term Debt to Net Working Capital. This ratio provides an insight into the ability of a firm to pay down long-term debt from current assets after pay down of current liabilities. A lower ratio is indicative of a stronger solvency position.

Long-Term Debt to Net Working Capital = Long-Term Debt
Net Working Capital

Efficiency Ratios - How well is your customer doing?

Efficiency ratios provide information about management's ability to control expenses and to earn a return on the resources committed to the business.

Cash Turnover. This ratio is a measure of how effectively a company utilizes its available cash. The higher the ratio the more efficiently a business is utilizing cash resources.

Cash Turnover = Net Sales
Cash

Sales to Net Worth. This ratio describes the rate at which tangible net worth is turned in the business and is a measure of management's ability to manage resources. It is desirable to utilize investor capital as actively as possible while maintaining a sound financial position.

Sales to Net Worth = Net Sales
Tangible Net Worth

Inventory Turnover. This relationship is a guide to the condition of inventories by showing the number of inventory is turned over (or sold) in the course of a year. For example if the ratio equals 2 it means that, on average, inventory turns over two times a year or every six months. Some credit managers use an average inventory figure for this calculation; they add beginning and ending inventories and divide by two. Others use ending inventory only. Still others relate inventory to the cost of goods sold. Regardless of which method is used, it is important to apply it consistently when analyzing the figures of successive years for any company.

Inventory Turnover = Cost of Goods Sold
Average Inventory

Accounts Receivable Turnover. Accounts receivable turnover measures the efficiency with which company resources are employed in accounts receivable. A high number indicates rapid turnover (collection) of funds, while a low one might reflect slow collections, granting of special terms, seasonal variations in selling patterns or an unexpected sharp rise in the volume of business.

Accounts Receivable Turnover = Net Sales
Average Gross Receivables

Profitability Measures - Is your customer turning sales into income?

Profitability Measures show the yield to your customers business of particular financial resources.

Operating Income Margin. This ratio measures the return on volume and is useful for gauging the effectiveness of management. If the figure is small in comparison to industry standards, you should examine the income statement for the cause of the modest return. Maybe the salary scale for management is too high, selling expenses are too high, or a nonrecurring item such as a bad-debt write-off was responsible for the low rate of return.

30

$$\text{Operating Income Margin} = \frac{\text{Operating Income}}{\text{Net Sales}}$$

Return on Equity. This relationship measures the rate of return on equity. It complements the operating income margin as a tool for gauging the effectiveness of management, since it reflects the efficiency with which owner's interest is used in the business.

$$\text{Return on Equity} = \frac{\text{Net Income}}{\text{Equity}}$$

Return on Assets. This relationship measures a company's ability to utilize its assets to create profits. It too can be used as a complementary ratio to operating income margin and demonstrates management's ability to gain efficiencies through efficient asset management.

$$\text{Return on Assets} = \frac{\text{Net Income}}{\text{Assets}}$$

How should I use trend analysis?

This technique enables you to determine the trend of operations by comparing a current financial statement with two or more prior statements of the same customer. Trend analysis can mix interim statements with annual figures, but comparing successive annual financial statements of the same calendar date eliminates seasonal variations in the figures. The same auditing technique and presentation should be employed on all statements, and changes in valuation basis and treatment of individual items should be explained.

Balance Sheet Trends. Item-by-item comparison of two or more successive balance sheets of the same customer will give definite information on the trend of the business and the direction and velocity of change. Individual balance sheet items and ratios will vary considerably with the season, volume changes, collections and payments, and the ordinary daily activities of a business.

Income Statement Trends. The component items of the income statement can also be compared year to year for trends in the financial operations. The trend of sales is an indication of growth and progress. Variations in cost of goods sold and gross profit are considered a measure of management's ability to maintain a competitive advantage. Controlling expenses also determines management's ability to create efficiencies. Finally, a steady increase in net earnings from year to year is a favorable sign.

31

Statement of Changes in Financial Position. Careful study of this worksheet will point out any disproportionate buildup of asset items and how they were financed. It will also show the extent to which liabilities were liquidated and the source of funds used to reduce those liabilities. Changes in net working capital are examined by reviewing the variations that have taken place in assets, liabilities and equity. The objective is to determine shifts in the magnitudes of current and non-current assets, short-term and long-term debt and equity components. Later, when dollar amounts have been established, the individual items can be reviewed to note their separate impacts on the composition of net working capital.

Should you use industry standards to see how your customer stacks up against competition?

Analysis of a company's financial statement will provide you with a lot of information on the financial condition of the company. However without looking at the industry as a whole, some of the information may be hard to interpret. Comparing one company's statement or ratios with the statement or ratios of other companies in the same industry or operating under similar conditions, can provide you with a good frame of reference in evaluating the data.

Percentage Statements. These provide a helpful analytical tool that strives to eliminate complete reliance on organizational size by reducing balance sheet and income statement components to percentages. Every asset item in the balance sheet is shown as a percentage of total assets. Likewise, every liability and stockholders' equity item is shown as a percentage of the total of liabilities and stockholders' equity. In the income statement, every income and expense item is shown as a percentage of total sales.

There are two types of percentage statements: Composite and pattern statements. Net sales is usually the base for operating data in both composite and pattern statements.

Composite statements, also called common size, are merely averages arrived at by combining financial statements of many organizations within the industry with no regard to size or condition of individual firms.

Pattern statements are also comprised of average figures but they are compiled on a more selective and refined basis than composite statements. In some pattern statements, items are related to total assets, total liabilities and stockholders' equity; while in others, the items may be related to other bases, such as tangible net worth or net working capital.

Sources of Financial Statement Standards. A number of sources provide statement norms for almost every field of business in which credit is extended. Credit agencies, bankers and industry associations, in particular, are in a position to assemble sufficient statements for this purpose. Credit departments of large companies can provide comparable data on their own customers by careful selection and combining of customers' statements; these figures would have the advantage of reflecting the seller company's policy because they would be made up of customers that have been approved. The Risk Management Association, as well as Dun & Bradstreet, publishes composite financial data on many lines of business, generally according to company size.

Financial Statement Analysis

Chapter Summary

This Chapter Answers the Following Questions:

- What is financial statement analysis?
- How do you determine the reliability of the financial data?
- What are the Balance Sheet, the Income Statement and the Statement of Changes in Financial Position?
- What type of internal analysis should I perform?
  - Liquidity Ratios
  - Solvency Ratios
  - Efficiency Ratios
  - Profitability Measures
- How should I use Trend Analysis?
- Should you use Industry Standards to see how your customer stacks up against competition?

Key Points:

- A key component to the credit decision-making process is the financial analysis of the customer's financial condition.
- Analysis of a financial statement may be divided into two general categories: internal and comparative.
  - Internal analysis uses figures from the financial statements of a given date or period.
  - Comparative analysis may be used to determine trends when two or more successive sets of figures are reviewed, or may be used to evaluate a given company's financial statement against industry standards.
- Before you begin your analysis of the financial statements, you should assess the reliability of the financial data. There are four basic types of financial statements: audited, reviewed, compiled and management prepared.
- The Balance Sheet provides a snapshot of the financial condition at a given point in time. It is a statement of assets, liabilities and net worth.
- The Income Statement shows sales, cost of goods sold, gross profit, expenses, net operating income, other income and expenses, federal income taxes, and net income.
- The Statement of Changes in Financial Position can be most useful for analyzing financial strength. It presents financial information in two

separate parts; sources and uses of funds and statement of cash flows.

➢ The major tools for internal analysis are balance sheet ratios and a working knowledge of the line of business, including the method of operation and seasonal influences.

➢ Ratio analyses make it possible to determine if asset and liability relationships are reasonably aligned. They measure liquidity, solvency, efficiency and profitability.

➢ Trend analysis enables you to determine the trend of operations by comparing a current financial statement with two or more prior statements of the same concern.

➢ Analysis of a company's financial statement will provide you with a lot of information on the financial condition of the company. However without looking at the industry as a whole, some of the information may be hard to interpret. Comparing one companies statement or ratios with the statement or ratios of other companies in the same industry or operating under similar conditions, can provide you with a good frame of reference in evaluating the data.

➢ Percentage Statements provide a helpful analytical tool that strives to eliminate complete reliance on organizational size by reducing balance sheet and income statement components to percentages.

COLLECTION PROCEDURES

The statement that a sale is not complete until the cash is in the bank is both familiar and true. A business organization would soon run out of operating capital if it were not continuously replenished through collection of its receivables. Unless receivables are converted to cash on schedule, some of the company assets are unproductively tied up. Companies that allow customers to become past due encounter this situation. Additionally, as a result, your condition may become restricted and interfere with your own ability to pay bills on time. This neglect of financial principles could affect your company's reputation in the trade and may even lead to financial embarrassment.

What should you consider when establishing the collection process?

The principles found especially useful by those experienced in the field of collection may be grouped into four areas: collect the money, maintain a systematic follow-up, get the customer to discuss the account, and preserve good will.

Collect the Money. The prime job of the people responsible for collections is to collect the money as close to the selling terms as possible. Your customer has an obligation to pay invoices within terms. It is the job of the collector to make sure that this obligation is met. The tone may be easy at first, but it should be stiffened and accelerated as much as necessary to ensure payment of the delinquent account.

Systematic Follow-up. After the initial contact with a delinquent account, it is important to keep additional contacts on a strict schedule. For instance, if you are told that a partial payment (not always acceptable) will be mailed in a few days, that information should be noted. If the check is not received at the promised time, a follow-up is essential. Otherwise, the collection effort may become ineffective.

Systematic follow-up indicates to your delinquent debtor the importance attached to the delinquent dollar amount by the creditor. That in itself creates an important collection advantage.

Get the Customer to Discuss the Account. Once you get the customer to talk about its delinquency situation, you are well on the way toward receiving payment. That is why emphasis is placed on inviting the customer to talk. The request to respond may be made by mail, phone, email, fax, or in person.

The object of the discussion is to get your customer's explanation of the delinquency. It may be a question of faulty merchandise; there may be issues regarding lack of compliance with customer requirements, it may be due to a temporary shortage of funds; or they may intend to hold off payment so the creditor's money can be used in its own business.

Preserve Good Will. Although a customer may currently be having trouble meeting payments, it does not preclude the account from becoming a good customer in the future. It is, therefore, important for you to preserve the customer's good will while pressing for collection. This requires not only tact, but also knowledge of the account.

However, if a choice has to be made between collecting the money and preserving good will, usually the emphasis should be placed on collecting the money. A customer that does not intend to pay legitimate debts is not to be considered a desired account.

Who should assume the collection responsibility?

In a small business operated by one person, it is obvious who is responsible for collections. Many proprietors personally attend to the collection of accounts. Their efforts are effective because they are well aware of the need for continual replenishment of operating capital.

In larger businesses, where the collection responsibility should rest depends on the nature of the company's organization. Generally, the larger the company, the farther the collection function is removed from the chief executive officer or owner. In medium or small-sized companies, one of the officers, most frequently the Controller or Treasurer is charged with the collection responsibility. In fact, even in larger organizations where the responsibility for collection is one of the specified functions of the credit department, higher management closely follows the success with which the function is carried out.

Your sales organization has a continuing stake in the collection function, and cooperation between the salesperson and the collector for the purpose of reducing the account's indebtedness will help to achieve organizational goals. Keeping the sales representative informed of the status of customer accounts by means of copies of statements, collection letters, or other correspondence flowing between the collector and the customer is generally more effective in promoting cooperation and enhances the understanding of mutual problems.

Sometimes a salesperson can handle collections more easily on the spot than the collector can at a distance. If the sales person discovers that the customer may be having financial difficulty, it should be brought to the attention of management immediately, so that appropriate arrangements may be made between your company and your customer.

 It should be noted that the primary job of the sales representative is to sell. While the salesperson is frequently in a position to act on behalf of the company to collect past due obligations, it should be left up to the salesperson to determine if the customer can be approached without an impact to the goodwill that has been established between the sales representative and the delinquent customer. Establishing a dependence on the salesperson to act as a collector is generally not a prudent approach.

What should the collection effort entail?

Awareness is the first step in collections--awareness of what is happening in the economy, in your industry, in your own company, and with your customer. The same investigative and analytical techniques, which are used for credit approval, are valid for the collection process. Unless you have some idea of what your customer's problems may be and why they are paying you slowly (or not paying at all), you may not take the correct first crucial step in collection.

The collection process begins with finance, and then with other areas of your organization, such as shipping, billing, sales and service. Before contacting the customer, make sure you clear up any internal process problems such as:

- Unapplied checks
- Unresolved billing, merchandise, or compliance disputes
- Unused or un-issued credits for returns or adjustments
- Any verbal "special terms" given by sales reps

The actual collection procedure begins with the impending maturity of an open invoice. The question then centers upon when the initial collection contact will be made. That is, how long after the due date will the collection process begin? Your basic policy should also specify the timing of the second and subsequent follow-ups, if the initial effort does not facilitate payment of the past-due amount. In considering the timing, it is necessary to consider the distances involved and the time required for an exchange of mail, the total number of follow-ups, the personnel available to handle them, and the practical matter of giving customers a reasonable time to respond to the collection effort.

For proper control, it is important to keep a clear record of accounts that have remained open beyond the regular terms of sale and are past due. The choice of a specific collection system will probably be determined by the basic accounting system used in invoicing customers and ledgering accounts receivable. In most organizations, automation is used to prepare statements and to write collection letters.

Statements of Account. A simple statement of account, listing the invoices outstanding and due for payment, is widely used in the initial collection effort. Usually it is sent without a message, but sometimes it carries a simple and courteous request for payment. A statement of account should include sufficient basic information, such as the customer's purchase order number, to permit a customer to check it readily against its own records prior to sending a remittance.

Early Stages of Collection. The essential factor in any collection effort is to use a procedure that is most effective from the standpoint of time and expense. Depending upon customer characteristics, this may be computer-generated letters, individually prepared letters, copies of invoices, or telephone calls.

➤ Computer generated form letters provide substantial savings in time and expense. However, they are not too effective with seriously delinquent accounts due to the fact that the recipient recognizes it as nothing more than an automated communication. Computer generated letters list past-due invoices and ask for payment. The message portion will vary depending upon which letter of a series is being sent.

➤ Individually prepared collection letters serve the same purpose as the form letter, but convey a message to the recipient that a collector is aware of the delinquency and will likely take further action if payment is not forthcoming. This letter should be as brief as possible and identify the items that have become past due.

➤ Copies of invoices are used with large national accounts because they provide more information than that shown on statements of accounts and collection letters.

➤ Direct telephone contact is the preferred method with high-risk accounts where sizable amounts are owing. This approach, if handled properly, helps establish better understanding, accelerates the collection of delinquent receivables, builds good will and may have an impact on increasing sales.

Intermediate Stages of Collection. Customers not responding to early collection efforts present real problems and pose a challenge to the collector's ability. The frequency of contact in the intermediate stage will vary according to the period of time an organization deems appropriate as detailed in its collection procedures policy. It will also be affected by the condition of the customer's account. This makes it imperative that the collector be thoroughly familiar with the credit facts of the account. The follow-up intervals must be maintained on a regular basis; it is usually considered good business to allow a period of 10 to 15 days between collection contacts.

Intermediate collection efforts are generally handled by correspondence, although there is a definite place for telephone conversations or personal visits if the expense is justified by the amount involved. At this stage, the collector's full abilities must be applied in writing resourceful, appealing and tactful letters that induce the customer to clear the obligation without impairing good will.

Intermediate collection letters generated through an automated process can have the message portion tailor-made. Consequently, they are usually successful, especially when combined with telephone calls that make the customer increasingly aware of the creditor's concern. Psychological appeals may be made to the customer's spirit of cooperation or the idea of maintaining a good credit record.

During this process it is quite common for customers to promise payment, give excuses for nonpayment, or send partial remittances to be applied on their account. Such responses give the collector something to work on. Common sense and good business judgment will assist the collector to set up specific dates and amounts or some type of agreement that will lead to complete payment at the earliest possible date.

Guided by these basic principles, each individual must develop skills and adeptness through experience. The approach that works with one customer may fail with another, but experience will help the collector develop certain techniques that prove repeatedly effective and can be used indefinitely.

Final Stages of Collection. When normal procedures fail to bring in the money and it is concluded that outside assistance or legal action may be necessary, collection activities reach the final stage. The length of time between the intermediate and final stages differs from one business to another. Terms of sale, customs within an industry, and general economic conditions facing a customer must be taken into consideration. Again, the credit file must be reviewed to make certain that the latest information is included before the decision to engage a third party is made.

The final collection effort is designed to motivate seriously past-due customers to pay their account and thereby avoid the cost of forced settlement through a third-party action. The most effective letters point out in a businesslike manner that further delay can be permitted only if the debtor makes definite and immediate arrangements for settlement, the alternative implication being a costly legal action. The goal at this point is to get action, to make the debtor pay immediately, or stand the expense and involvement of a third party action. When the use of third party assistance is indicated, and the delinquent account fails to respond, the account should be referred to a third party collection agency or attorney.

What steps should be taken when referring a delinquent account to a third party?

When internal collection efforts have been exhausted, it frequently becomes prudent to refer the collection to outside collection sources. They can be extremely helpful, but should be selected with care. Although your customer has failed to settle their account, you as the creditor may still have a desire to maintain goodwill and to make future sales to the customer on a cash basis. Therefore, careful consideration should be given to the kind of impression third parties may make on the customer.

Collection Agencies. Prior to referring an account to a third party collection agency you should have a thorough understanding of who the agency is. References should be obtained and an awareness of the agencies reputation and its ability to handle the job properly should be sought. Fee structures should be negotiated and agreed upon in writing prior to placing the initial account for collection. Usually charges are contingent upon collection. Accounts that are deemed as uncollectible by the agency are generally returned after the collection has been attempted. A full report of the steps taken in the collection effort should accompany the returned accounts.

(Note: A good source for helping you find a certified collection agency is the Commercial Collection Agency Association of the Commercial Law League of America (www.ccascollect.com). They can help you identify those agencies that provide competent, quality collections and insolvency services.)

Collection by Attorneys. Instead of using a collection agency, you can submit a delinquent account to an attorney for appropriate action. It is wise to select an attorney within the customer's community who may be in a better position to win the customer's confidence and work out some form of settlement. If the delinquent customer does not respond, the attorney has the additional advantage of being able to institute legal action in the local jurisdiction immediately.

If legal action is necessary, it must be taken while the debtor has assets in its possession. In the event of business failure, receivership, foreclosure, or bankruptcy, the assistance of an attorney should be sought at least until you are sufficiently experienced to know which of these circumstances you can safely address yourself.

Seriously delinquent accounts should be considered for write-off as bad debts or transferred to the suspense ledger in some nominal amount to ensure continued follow-up until finally settled. Where some real possibility of collection exists, follow-up should be continued until the account is deemed as totally uncollectible.

Documentation for Third Party Collection. When you turn an account over for collection, you should give the agency or attorney a complete package that includes the following documentation:

- A statement of all charges.

- Copies of purchase orders, invoices, proofs of delivery, contracts, etc.

- Photocopies of customer's checks for any partial payments.

- Any correspondence sent or received on any of the outstanding items together with any claims of shortages, non-conforming goods, breakage or returns.

- Copies of any personal or corporate guarantees and/or any security agreements, along with copies of any UCC forms showing the dates filed.

The more back-up detail the agency or attorney has, the better they can work for you. If the matter has to go to suit, you would have to provide this information anyway, so you might as well do it at the beginning of the process. If paperwork to support litigation is missing, you will have the time to locate it.

Your Role in the Process. Unless there is a good reason for you to become involved (e.g., a return of merchandise or a valid claim which reduces the amount owing, and requires you to issue a credit memo) do not interfere with the process between your customer and the agency or attorney. You hired them; so let them do their job. Many times a customer will contact you and try to negotiate a settlement so they won't have to pay collection charges or have their reputation tarnished. At this juncture it is important to realize that you made a conscious decision to outsource the collection of the account to the third party. Stand firm and insist to the customer that they need to negotiate with the agency or attorney. Don't encumber the process by intervening, thus running the risk of thwarting the third party effort.

Collection Procedures

Chapter Summary

This Chapter Answers the Following Questions:

➢ What should you consider when establishing the collection process?

➢ Who should assume the collection responsibility?

➢ What should the collection effort entail?

➢ What steps should be taken when referring a delinquent account to a third party?

Key Points:

➢ The statement that a sale is not complete until the cash is in the bank is both familiar and true. A business organization would soon run out of operating capital if it were not continuously replenished through collection of its receivables.

➢ Collection principles may be grouped into four areas: collect the money, maintain a systematic follow-up, get the customer to discuss the account, and preserve good will.

➢ In medium or small-sized companies, one of the officers, most frequently the Controller or Treasurer is charged with overseeing the collection responsibility.

➢ The essential factor in any collection effort is to use a procedure that is most effective from the standpoint of time and expense. Depending upon customer characteristics, this may be computer-generated letters, individually prepared letters, copies of invoices, or telephone calls.

➢ Intermediate collection efforts are generally handled by correspondence, although there is a definite place for telephone conversations or personal visits, if the expense is justified by the amount involved.

➢ The final collection effort is designed to motivate seriously past-due customers to pay their account and thereby avoid the cost of forced settlement through a third-party action.

➢ When internal collection efforts have been exhausted, it frequently becomes prudent to refer the collection to outside collection sources such as a third party collection agency or attorney. They can be extremely helpful but should be selected with care.

➢ Seriously delinquent accounts should be considered for write off as bad debts or transferred to the suspense ledger in some nominal amount to ensure continued follow-up until finally settled.

DOING BUSINESS WITH A DISTRESSED CUSTOMER

One of the unfortunate consequences of selling on open credit terms is that it is inevitable that the day will come when you discover that a customer is not able to pay you. This is typically due to the fact that its business has become distressed and it has insufficient capital to meet all of its obligations. To prepare for this occurrence it is important that you gain a general understanding of what circumstances contribute to a distressed business and what remedy you have as a creditor to recover monies from a distressed debtor.

What are the reasons for financial distress?

It could be argued that creditors often willingly, but probably unknowingly, cooperated in permitting the debtor to become distressed. Frequently, lax credit analysis and poor collection follow-up contribute to the bad business habits of many customers, and foster distress. There are typically four potential reasons for business distress:

> Businesses that are under-capitalized and consequently rely on their creditors' capital to pull them through.

> Businesses who sustain losses because of declines in customer demand.

> Businesses who become inefficient because they failed to adapt advanced processes or technology.

> Businesses that are poorly managed, or victimized by fraud on the part of senior management.

What are my options in dealing with a financially distressed business that owes me money?

The methods of handling the affairs of financially distressed or insolvent business debtors may be divided into two classes: those designed to keep the debtor in business and restore the business to profitability; and those designed to put the debtor out of business, realize the assets, and distribute the proceeds among creditors.

Insolvency as defined by the Bankruptcy Code is based on the traditional balance sheet test in which debts exceed assets, at fair value. However, a debtor does not have to show insolvency to be granted relief under the Bankruptcy Code. To place a debtor into an involuntary bankruptcy, you need not prove insolvency. You need only to demonstrate that the debtor is not paying its debts as they come due.

Out-Of-Court Settlements. Creditors usually prefer to rehabilitate or work with a distressed debtor through voluntary, out-of-court settlements. When rehabilitation is not possible, they may liquidate assets outside of bankruptcy proceedings through a general assignment for the benefit of creditors or an agreement to liquidate between creditors and the debtor. The credit person who is familiar with both of these methods, their requirements, advantages and disadvantages, will be able to participate effectively and intelligently in whatever action is taken when a customer becomes insolvent.

Voluntary settlements between debtors and creditors are the preferred answer to the resolution of a financial problem. These settlements are commonly referred to as "general compositions" and "extension agreements". Composition agreements are usually those that allow the debtor to pay less than 100% of what is due. An extension agreement is one that allows the debtor to pay over an extended period of time. Frequently an agreement includes both a composition and an extension, and provides for rehabilitation of the debtor and for its continuance in business. These agreements generally require the acceptance of approximately 90% of the creditors.

Expressed in another way, a voluntary settlement is simply a contract between the debtor and creditors that settles their claims to maximize the return for the creditors, while minimizing the financial distress of the debtor. It keeps the customer in business and avoids unnecessary court costs. The creditors may take a temporary loss, but expect the debtor to emerge stable and solvent.

Some advantages of an out-of-court settlement to the debtor include:
> Less negative publicity in the legal and business community.
> Less time consuming and usually less expensive than a formal bankruptcy proceeding.
> Less interruption in the conduct of the debtor's business.
> Greater certainty of control by the debtor of business operations.
> Less risk in losing a management team and skilled labor.
> Greater flexibility for cash flow control.
> Avoidance of triggering default clauses in leases and security agreements.
> Better atmosphere for refinancing, capital infusion or new borrowing.
> Sale or lease of assets is less cumbersome particularly those out of the ordinary course of business.

➢ Less possibility of reduction in salary and other benefits paid to key employees.

➢ Greater protection of confidential business matters.

Some disadvantages of an out-of court settlement to the debtor include:

➢ No protection against secured parties, judicial, or statutory lien creditors seeking to enforce their rights pursuant to written agreements with the debtor.

➢ No ability to halt action by taxing authority.

➢ Inability to stay (halt) state or federal court proceedings pending against debtor or which may be initiated against the debtor after the agreement is initiated.

➢ Inability to reject collective bargaining agreements with employees.

➢ Inability to sell or transfer assets, free and clear of liens and encumbrances, with the exception of the agreements with all lien claimants.

➢ Inability to reject leases and other burdensome executory contracts.

➢ Unavailability of bankruptcy "cramdown" provisions to deal with under secured creditors' claims.

➢ Unavailability of a forum for prompt resolution of disputes affecting the debtor.

➢ Difficult mechanism for allowance of attorney's fees for the counsel of various parties or a forum for resolution of disputes regarding payment of professionals.

➢ No mechanism to attack preferential transfers, fraudulent conveyances or attachments, etc. of the debtor's property.

➢ No legal way to compel dissenting creditors to cooperate with settlement.

The substantial utilization of the out-of-court settlement is ample proof of its wide acceptance by sophisticated creditors and attorneys who specialize in the law of insolvency. The benefits derived from the out-of-court settlement have been recognized in the Bankruptcy Code by the enactment of section 305, which permits the Bankruptcy Court to abstain an involuntary petition in bankruptcy filed against a debtor if the dismissal would better serve the interest of the creditors and the debtor. A well-constructed out-of-court settlement agreement between a debtor and a representative body of its creditors stands an excellent chance of serving its purpose.

The Meeting of Creditors. If the decision has been made to attempt an out-of-court settlement, usually the debtor's counsel may analyze the list of the twenty (or other suitable, representative number) largest creditors with an eye towards identifying those creditors who might be helpful as well as those who might be a stumbling block to working out an agreement. The first meeting of the creditors can be a confusing affair or it can be well organized depending on the preparation of the debtors and the creditors. Ideally, the debtor will come to the meeting accompanied by both its counsel and accountant. The debtor will have current financial statements, be prepared to give the entire financial history of the business as well as the reasons for its distressed condition, and be able to answer creditors' questions.

At this first meeting of creditors, consideration should be given to electing a creditors' committee designed to be representative of all the creditors with whom the debtor will negotiate an agreement.

The committee should be formed based on those creditors who are willing to participate. After the committee has been formed, it should retain a secretary to keep minutes of the meeting, furnish the creditors with status reports of the committees' deliberations, provide for the distribution of the agreement to the creditors, and seek consensus on the part of all creditors to the agreement.

The committee should also retain counsel in the formation and preparation of the agreement with the debtor. When facts and circumstances warrant, the committee should retain an accountant other than the one employed by the debtor to conduct an independent investigation of the debtor's financial affairs and review, if not audit, its books and records.

The Composition Agreement. This type of settlement proposes to settle with creditors for less than the full amounts owed. The debtor pays to its creditors a uniform percentage of its obligations to be accepted in full settlement. The percentage depends upon what the debtor's assets are, what the debtor is able to pay, and what the creditors are able to negotiate in the bargaining proceedings. Sometimes the debtor may obtain third party financing to make an attractive settlement with creditors.

The most important criterion in determining a fair settlement is to compare the proposal to an estimated settlement in bankruptcy or liquidation. A pro rata voluntary settlement should provide a larger dividend than would result in bankruptcy proceedings or liquidation. It is often advisable to provide creditors of small claims (relative to the situation) with payment in full to reduce the number of creditors and eliminate the nuisance those small

47

claims can cause. Furthermore, it may be wise to provide that creditors agreeing to reduce their claims to a specified amount will receive 100% of their adjusted claims.

Extension Agreements. Perhaps the least drastic method of dealing with a distressed debtor who cannot pay its bills is by the acceptance of an extension agreement. Under this agreement the time for payment of accounts is legally postponed to some future date mutually agreed upon by the debtor and its creditors.

Considerations on the part of creditors in accepting an extension agreement include:

> ➢ The honesty of the debtor.
> ➢ Determination of whether the extension will accomplish its purpose.
> ➢ Does the debtor have sufficient financial strength available?
> ➢ Is the debtor competent?

 It should be noted that creditors are not compelled to sign a composition or extension agreement, and creditors who do not sign it are not bound by it.

The Combination Settlement. Combination settlements usually call for a pro rata cash payment combined with an extension of time. For example, the settlement may provide a cash payment of 20% and three future installments of 5% each, for a total of 35% in full settlement. The installment payments, usually evidenced by notes, may be payable at 3, 6, 9, or 12 month intervals. The disbursements are usually made by an attorney for the creditors rather than by the debtor.

Assignment for the Benefit of Creditors. While the creditors' efforts are ordinarily directed toward rehabilitating the distressed debtor, some debtors are so hopelessly insolvent and lacking in prospects that they cannot be rehabilitated. In those cases, the debtor may be asked to execute a general assignment for the benefit of creditors, a liquidation technique by which the debtor goes out of business. The assignment is a device whereby a debtor transfers title to all assets to a third party, designated as assignee or trustee, with instructions to liquidate the assets and distribute the proceeds among creditors on a pro rata basis. A debtor may make the assignment without prior consultation with the creditors, or it may be executed after meetings with creditors or a creditors' committee when it becomes obvious that a voluntary settlement cannot be made. As a creditor, you must file a claim as stipulated by the assignee. In most cases, that is the only way you will be paid. One caveat must be considered in an assignment; that is the assets to be assigned must be unencumbered. With lenders and some vendors taking a more secured position in recent years, the assignment has diminished in popularity.

Liquidation Agreement. Liquidation can also be undertaken by a consenting agreement between the distressed debtor and the creditors to convert the assets of the business and distribute the proceeds according to the agreement, among the creditors. Creditors should be supported by an attorney who can act as a point-person to represent all creditors, and can (on the consent of the creditors' committee), prepare all documentation to ensure an equitable distribution.

Receivership Proceedings (a non-bankruptcy, court proceeding). Unlike compositions and assignments for the benefit of creditors, receivership proceedings are rarely voluntary. In most states, receivership proceedings can only be instituted by the commencement of an adversary-type proceeding, and the receivership is instituted only after the court has made the determination that it is necessary and proper.

Each state can have different rules governing receivership administration, therefore careful attention should be paid by creditors to all communication received in the case so that they can maximize their return. If creditors feel that the state is not looking out for their best interest, it is possible to consider filing an involuntary bankruptcy case against the debtor to control the situation in either a Chapter 7 or 11.

Bankruptcy--the formal proceeding. An overall understanding of formal proceedings is essential for the credit professional so that as the situation arises, you can be conversant and knowledgeable of some things you can and cannot do while your customer is under the jurisdiction of the Bankruptcy Court. The Bankruptcy Code is the aggregate law that dictates the actions of all parties involved in the case.

What should I know about Bankruptcy?

There are two primary Chapters of the bankruptcy code that govern commercial bankruptcy filings. These are *Chapter 7 and Chapter 11*.

Chapter 7. This provision contains the framework for an ordinary liquidation proceeding. It is the "straight bankruptcy" chapter and provides for appointment of an interim trustee; election and duties of a trustee;

election of a creditors' committee; the collection, liquidation and distribution of the assets of the estate; and the discharge of the debtor.

This action petitions the court for immediate liquidation, and the business closes its door. The business assets are inventoried, appraised, and liquidated; the proceeds are distributed first to secured creditors, and then on a pro rata basis to unsecured creditors after administrative expenses and other priority claims including taxes, etc. are paid. In most cases, other than filing a claim with the court, there is little else for a commercial credit grantor to do. The amount unsecured creditors receive, if anything, is usually very small. In most cases, even the secured creditors do not realize 100% on their claims. On rare occasions, Chapter 7 cases may be converted to Chapter 11 if the court agrees that creditors may receive a higher payout if the business attempts reorganization. It should be noted that a debtor could convert an involuntary Chapter 7 at will.

Chapter 11. The primary purpose of this Chapter is to promote the rehabilitation and the continued viability of the debtor. A Chapter 11 plan may, however, provide for the orderly liquidation of the debtor.

Under this chapter, proprietorships, partnerships and corporations attempt to gain breathing space, while they work with creditors to reorganize their finances and arrange a payment plan to which creditors will agree. This is called a Plan of Reorganization, allowing the debtor to be in possession of its assets (Debtor in Possession or DIP). A major difference between this and Chapter 7 is that the business intends to continue to operate after the Chapter 11 proceedings have concluded.

The filing of a Chapter 11 is usually preceded by events such as an actual or threatened foreclosure on fixed assets or inventory by a secured creditor; a large number of suits filed by unsecured creditors; the refusal of a lender to continue a line of credit; or the falling apart of an out-of-court settlement.

Once the court accepts the petition, it prohibits all creditors, even those secured or with judgments, from taking any additional collection or legal action. This restriction, known as the "automatic stay," continues until the court rules otherwise. The court sends notices to all known creditors, and schedules a first meeting of creditors known as a 341 meeting (Section 341 of the Bankruptcy Code). A creditors' committee, which normally includes the seven largest unsecured creditors and others that the court may appoint, is formed to help investigate, review, and analyze all pertinent financial and operating information. It helps the court determine if the debtor has given an honest and full financial disclosure, if the continuance of the business appears feasible, and it helps to devise or recommend a plan of arrangement offered by the debtor. If a very large company whose finances are heavily involved with many classes of creditors files a petition, the court may appoint more than one creditors' committee.

Shortly after the first meeting of creditors, the court may appoint a trustee approved by the creditors to oversee the operations of the debtor and the overall proceedings when improprieties may be suspected. As part of this process, frequent detailed reports must be filed by the debtor, so the trustee can determine that company's management is operating the company prudently, not further dissipating assets, and is abiding by any court-ordered restrictions.

While the debtor has the sole right to propose a plan of arrangement for the 120 days after the filing of the petition, more often than not this period is extended by the court for several months. After the 120-day period (or extensions), the creditors may put forth their own plan.

While negotiations are going on, the court, in addition to tending to legal matters of the case, processes all the claims filed by unsecured creditors. There is a deadline for filing claims. This is sometimes referred to as the "bar date," and is usually included in the filing notice sent to creditors.

The debtor may file an action to expunge or reduce a creditor's claim through its attorney. Failure to object to the debtor's motion will cause a creditor's claim to be expunged or reduced as motioned by the debtor. Accordingly, action should be taken immediately to object to the debtor's motion with supporting documents verifying the creditor's claim attached thereto.

After the creditors' committee approves the plan of arrangement, copies are sent to creditors for their review. Prior to, or accompanying the plan, a "disclosure statement" which contains sufficient background and financial information to allow the creditors to make an informed decision about the plan, is submitted to the creditors. If more than 50% of the number of unsecured creditors whose claims collectively represent two-thirds of the dollar amount of unsecured claims vote for the plan, the plan is confirmed.
After confirmation, the debtor is "discharged" from bankruptcy, which for practical purposes means that management takes back the operations of the company as long as the terms of the plan of arrangement are met.

If the creditors do not approve a plan of arrangement, the court may still approve it, if the bankruptcy judge believes it is in the best interest of all parties. This is known as the "cramdown" feature.

If a plan is not approved, or if at anytime during the Chapter 11 the court believes the debtor staying in business does not serve the best interests of creditors, the action can be converted to Chapter 7 and the business liquidated.

Small Business Chapter 11. Under the Bankruptcy Reform Act of 1994, a "small business" provision was adopted to permit an accelerated Chapter 11 for commercial or business debtors with less than $2,000,000 in debt. Debtors whose primary assets and operations relate to real estate are not eligible. In a "Small Business" case, the court may order that no creditors' committee be appointed, thereby saving expenses, but potentially minimizing the ability of creditors to have a meaningful influence in the case. Only the debtor may file a Chapter 11 plan and disclosure statement in the first 100 days. However, a plan must be filed by 160 days after the petition is filed. The court may combine the hearings on the disclosure statement and plan. Generally, the intent of the small business provision is to accelerate and streamline the Chapter 11 process in small cases.

How is a bankruptcy proceeding commenced?

There are several ways to commence a bankruptcy proceeding.

The Voluntary Petition. Voluntary proceedings are commenced by filing a petition under an applicable chapter of the Code as previously mentioned, by a party, which may be a debtor under that chapter. The petition is merely a brief written statement by the debtor, executed under oath.

The Involuntary Petition. An involuntary petition may be filed only against debtors actively engaged in business. They may be proprietorships, partnerships, or corporations; excluded are farmers and not-for-profit businesses. Likewise, involuntary relief is not available against municipalities under Chapter 9. It would simply be bad policy to allow a small number of creditors to control the fate of a municipality governed by popularly elected officials. Involuntary cases can only be commenced under Chapter 7 or Chapter 11 of the Bankruptcy Code under the following conditions:

If the debtor has less than twelve unsecured creditors, a single creditor holding at least $10,000.00 in unsecured claims can file or, if the debtor has more than twelve unsecured creditors of which three or more hold unsecured claims aggregating at least $10,000.00.

The Joint Petition. A joint case commences when an individual debtor and spouse file a single petition. A joint petition must be voluntary on the part of both parties; it is not possible for a debtor to drag his or her spouse into bankruptcy without the knowledge or consent of the latter. It must bear a sworn statement of both spouses that the petition is true.

The filing of a joint petition does not result in the automatic pooling of the assets and liabilities of the joint debtors. Rather, when presented with a joint petition, the court must determine the extent, if any, to which the debtor's estates should be consolidated.

How do I file my proof of claim in a bankruptcy?

When to File. In Chapter 11 cases, it is no longer required that the creditor file a Proof of Claim if the creditor recognizes its claim, *listed in an indisputable amount,* on the schedule of liabilities filed by the debtor. If however, there is any question or dispute about the amount listed (or if the creditor is not listed at all), the creditor must file a Proof of Claim in order to realize any settlement. *To be safe, always file a Proof of Claim in any bankruptcy proceeding.*

In a Chapter 7 all Proof of Claims must be filed within 90 days after the first date set for the § 341 meeting and will not be extended if the § 341 meeting is continued. If the 90th day falls on a weekend or holiday, the next business day is the deadline. In Chapter 11 bankruptcies, the bankruptcy court determines the deadline for filing the Proof of Claim.

(Note: An official proof of claim form may be obtained by accessing http://www.uscourts.gov/bankform/formb10new.pdf)

What are the priorities of claims in a bankruptcy settlement?

Secured Claimholders. Secured claimholders are entitled to payment prior to general claimholders to the extent of their secured interest.

Unsecured Claimholders. The following claims have priority, in the order listed, over other unsecured claims:
- ➢ All costs of administration, including all necessary expenses of preserving the estate, including wages, salaries, or commissions for services rendered after the commencement of the case.
- ➢ Any tax incurred by the estate.
- ➢ The expenses of creditors in recovering property for the benefit of the estate.

- ➢ Reasonable compensation for services of accountants and attorneys.
- ➢ In an involuntary case, unsecured claims arising out of the debtor's business after the commencement of the case, but before the appointment of the trustee.
- ➢ Wage claims up to $4,000 for each employee, including vacation, severance, and sick leave, earned in the 90 days before the earlier of the filing of the petition or the end of the debtor's business.
- ➢ Contributions to employee benefit plans.
- ➢ Unsecured consumer claims for deposits before the commencement of the case, in connection with the purchase, lease, or rental of property.
- ➢ Income taxes for which a return is due within three years of the commencement of the case, property taxes for one year, unemployment, or withholding.

What do I do if I am charged by the bankruptcy estate with having received a preferential payment?

The preference laws in a bankruptcy were designed to assure equal distribution of assets. They stipulate that any payment made by the debtor to a creditor within 90 days of a bankruptcy filing may have to be paid back to the bankruptcy estate prior to a distribution of assets. The trustee generally makes this determination. The law was designed to assure fair treatment to all creditors. If for example, a debtor determined there was a likelihood he would be forced to file for bankruptcy in the near future his natural inclination would be to satisfy financial obligations with family and friends with what limited assets he has. This course of action however, gives a certain class of creditors *(in this case family and friends)* an unfair advantage over other creditors. The preference laws were devised to prevent this from happening.

There will be times if you are involved with a bankruptcy of one of your customers that you may receive notice from a trustee requiring you to pay back monies that you had received within the 90 day period prior to the commencement of the bankruptcy. This tends to add insult to injury, because not only are you left with having to settle for a percentage of what is rightfully due to you, but also you are forced by law to pay additional monies back to the estate.

There are specific defenses designed to protect you in these situations. These are called preference defenses. Prior to paying any monies back to the bankruptcy estate, it is strongly recommended that you contact an attorney at once. In many cases the attorney is able to assist you in raising a defense against the preference action and creating a situation that relieves you of having to pay back the full amount of the preference claim.

What rights do I have to reclaim goods shipped to an insolvent customer?

The reclamation laws in bankruptcy were designed to provide relief to vendors who have in good faith made recent shipments of goods to a business that has become insolvent. The theory behind the creation of the law is to prevent a debtor, who has determined that it will file bankruptcy, from loading up on inventory prior to the filing and then avoiding payment for that inventory by virtue of the filing.

The law allows the creditor or merchandise supplier the opportunity to retrieve goods that were shipped within 10 days or in certain cases 20 days of the time the debtor became insolvent. *(Note – As of this writing the proposed Bankruptcy Reform Act of 2001 is pending before Congress. Under this law, if enacted, the reclamation period will be extended to 45 days, in certain cases.)*

To recover goods that have recently been shipped to an insolvent company it is imperative that you act immediately by contacting an attorney familiar with the bankruptcy process. The attorney can help you prepare the reclamation notice and advise you of the process you must follow to recover your goods.

DOING BUSINESS WITH A DISTRESSED CUSTOMER
Chapter Summary

This Chapter Answers the Following Questions:
➤ What are the reasons for financial distress?
➤ What are my options in dealing with a financially distressed business that owes me money?
➤ What should I know about Bankruptcy?
➤ How is a bankruptcy proceeding commenced?
➤ How do I file my proof of claim in a bankruptcy?
➤ What are the priorities of claims in a bankruptcy settlement?
➤ What do I do if I am charged by the bankruptcy estate with a preference?
➤ What rights do I have to reclaim goods shipped to an insolvent customer?

Key points:
➤ There are typically four potential reasons for business distress:
  - Businesses that are under-capitalized and consequently rely on their creditors' capital to pull them through.
  - Businesses who sustain losses because of declines in customer demand.
  - Businesses who become inefficient because they failed to adapt advanced processes or technology.
  - Businesses that are poorly managed, or victimized by fraud on the part of senior management.
➤ The methods of handling the affairs of financially distressed or insolvent business debtors may be divided into two classes: those designed to keep the debtor in business and restore the business to profitability; and those designed to put the debtor out of business, realize the assets, and distribute the proceeds among creditors.
➤ There are two primary Chapters of the bankruptcy code that govern commercial bankruptcy filings. These are Chapter 7 and Chapter 11.
  - The Chapter 7 provision contains the framework for an ordinary liquidation proceeding. It is the "straight bankruptcy" chapter and provides for appointment of an interim trustee; election and duties of a trustee; election of a creditors' committee; the collection, liquidation, and distribution of the assets of the estate; and the discharge of the debtor.

- The primary purpose of the Chapter 11 is to promote the rehabilitation and the continued viability of the debtor. A Chapter 11 plan may, however, provide for the orderly liquidation of the debtor.

➤ There are several ways to commence a bankruptcy proceeding.

- Voluntary Petition, Involuntary Petition and Joint Petition

➤ *Secured Claimholders.* Secured claimholders are entitled to payment prior to general claimholders to the extent of their secured interest.

➤ *Unsecured Claimholders.* The following claims have priority, in the order listed, over other unsecured claims:

- All costs of administration, including all necessary expenses of preserving the estate, including wages, salaries, or commissions for services rendered after the commencement of the case.

- Any tax incurred by the estate.

- The expenses of creditors in recovering property for the benefit of the estate.

- Reasonable compensation for services of accountants and attorneys.

- In an involuntary case, unsecured claims arising out of the debtor's business after the commencement of the case, but before the appointment of the trustee.

- Wage claims up to $4,000 for each employee, including vacation, severance, and sick leave, earned in the 90 days before the earlier of the filing of the petition or the end of the debtor's business.

- Contributions to employee benefit plans.

- Unsecured consumer claims for deposits before the commencement of the case, in connection with the purchase, lease, or rental of property.

- Income taxes for which a return is due within three years of the commencement of the case, property taxes for one year, unemployment, or withholding.

➤ There are specific defenses designed to protect you in the event of a preference action against you. These are called preference defenses. Prior to paying any monies back to the bankruptcy estate it is strongly recommended that you contact an attorney at once.

➤ To recover goods that have recently been shipped to an insolvent company it is imperative that you act immediately by contacting an attorney familiar with the reclamation laws.

EVALUATING YOUR RECEIVABLES PORTFOLIO

How do I track receivable performance?

Accounts receivables generally represent the largest liquid asset on the company balance sheet. Therefore, it is important to track the status of your organization's accounts receivable investment. You assess your organizations receivable performance on a monthly basis. It is not enough to focus on the favorable aspects, but you must also seek out the negatives and take remedial action to resolve them. In fact, you should identify the potential problems as early as possible and decide what needs to be done to resolve any issues.

The measure used by your company should convey the overall condition of the receivable investment. In selecting performance measures, the goal is to identify and use valid measures that will work over time, not just measures that work for the moment.

A meaningful measure should fill a need and meet your specific objectives. If a measure does not accomplish a purpose, don't use it. If a measure is being used and the objective is not understood, figure it out. Meaningful measures will support your organization's mission and help you reach organizational goals.

Some of the more commonly used measures of receivable performance include Aging of Accounts Receivable, Days Sales Outstanding, Best Possible Days Sales Outstanding, Average Days Delinquent and the Collection Effectiveness Index.

Aging of Accounts Receivable

This is a distribution of outstanding accounts, aged according to the periods they have been outstanding. The most common classification system is to age the receivables into the following aging "buckets": current, overdue 1 to 30 days, 31 to 60 days, 61 to 90 days and over 90 days. This keeps a clear-cut record of accounts that have remained open beyond their regular terms of sale. It helps to facilitate good collections and proper control of accounts.

These aging breakdowns are generally drawn from a monthly trial balance and should be made available at a regular monthly interval. Companies differ greatly in this practice depending upon the extent of their automation.

Days Sales Outstanding (DSO)

Days Sales Outstanding provides a convenient summary of your investment in receivables. It can be readily compared with your credit terms or similar standard. For example, if you sell on 30-day terms, you theoretically expect a complete turnover of receivables within 30 days and may act to stiffen collection procedures when the turnover period exceeds 30 days. As with other measures, this measure covers up the behavior of delinquent accounts when other accounts are paying their bills early. Marketing considerations such as extra dating (time to pay) could have an adverse impact on this measure. Additionally, because sales are a key variable in the equation, a rapid decline or run up in sales volume can skew the equation. Accordingly, this measure is not always the most accurate measure of collection performance. While this measure is most widely recognized as a measure of receivable performance, Average Day's Delinquent and the Collection Effectiveness Index serve as more accurate measures of collection performance, because they diminish the impact of the sales bias found in the DSO formula.

The CRF formula for calculating DSO is as follows:

<u>Average Receivables for Period Analyzed X Number of Days in Period</u>
Credit Sales for Period Analyzed

The average receivable balance is calculated by totaling the ending receivable balance for each month covered in the period and dividing that total by the number of months under consideration. The average receivable balance is used in the formula in order to smooth the data. If the balance at the end of the period were used, the DSO would be prone to move sharply up or down, particularly if the accounts receivable were abnormally high or low at the periods end. This would tend to create a saw-tooth effect on any DSO trend line being developed.

Best Possible DSO (BPDSO)

This figure expresses the best possible level of receivables. The measure calculates DSO on only that portion of the open receivable base that is current. In this calculation, all delinquent receivables are eliminated. The result reflects DSO assuming that there are no delinquent receivables. The outcome should approximate the standard selling terms. If terms for example are net 30 days, then the BPDSO should be at or near 30. Because credit sales are used as a variable in this calculation the same sales bias described in DSO exists in this calculation.

The formula for calculating BPDSO is as follows:

<u>Current Receivables X Number of Days in Period Analyzed</u>
Credit Sales for Period Analyzed

Average Days Delinquent (ADD)

This figure expresses in days, the average time from the invoice due date to the paid date, or the average days invoices are past due. Average Days Delinquent reflects the difference between DSO and Best possible DSO.

This calculation tends to mute some of the sales bias found in the DSO & BPDSO calculations.

The formula for calculating ADD is as follows:

Days Sales Outstanding - Best Possible Days Sales Outstanding

Collection Effectiveness Index (CEI)

This percentage expresses the effectiveness of collection efforts over time. The closer to 100 percent, the more effective the collection effort. It is a measure of the quality of the collection of receivables. The measure identifies what is available to collect and shows as a percent of what was available to collect what in fact was actually collected. This measure is generally regarded as the best measure of collection performance, because unlike DSO and BPDSO, it tends to mitigate the effect of the sales bias.

The formula for calculating CEI is as follows:

Beginning Receivables + Credit Sales/N* - Ending Total Receivables
Beginning Receivables + Credit Sales/N* - Ending Current Receivable

* N= the number of months in the period being considered

How do I manage my uncollectible accounts?

An important consideration usually associated with the collection responsibility is the maintenance of an allowance for uncollectible accounts. It is necessary to anticipate accounts that may prove uncollectible and then establish a reserve of profits to which such uncollectible accounts will ultimately be charged. It should be feasible to review your organization's collection experience as a start in determining how much of an allowance is needed. This involves a review of previous bad-debt write-offs and special problem accounts of substantial size that may have significant delinquency. In addition, the general trend of business conditions should be considered.

Allowance for Uncollectible Accounts. The individual most familiar with the delinquent accounts should make the initial calculations and recommendations for the allowance for uncollectible accounts. Accounts are commonly charged against the allowance for uncollectible accounts when it appears doubtful that collection can be made or when it is certain that only a portion of the total account outstanding can be recovered. Recoveries that may ultimately be obtained from diligent follow-up or litigation can be taken as a credit to the allowance for uncollectible accounts when they are received, whether in the current accounting period or at a later date.

Write-offs. Once an account is deemed to be uncollectible it should be removed from the company's books by charging it as a write-off to bad debt expense. A record of bad-debt losses should be maintained by every business, but it is dangerous to let this become the sole criterion of how good a job has been done in the management of the receivable portfolio. You must review the record of bad-debt losses in the light of profit margins, the goal of full production, and company plans to enter markets or expand operations with new products. A significant decline in bad debt write-offs may signal a situation where credit policy has become too restrictive thus encumbering sales growth. A rapid increase in bad debt write-offs could be indicative of too liberal a credit policy contributing to increased revenues at a cost to profitability.

To facilitate their use in industry and in product line comparisons, losses are generally shown net of the recoveries of prior years and expressed as a percentage of sales. The ratio typically pairs bad-debt losses originating in one period with sales of the following period. If there is a considerable delay in the recognition of losses, which frequently happens, any number of developments may impair the value of the ratio as a measure of effectiveness. An increase in sales, a change in credit policy, or a change in business conditions may alter successive figures to such an extent that they give no indication of your selectivity in extending credit during the period under consideration.

EVALUATING YOUR RECEIVABLES PORTFOLIO

Chapter Summary

This Chapter Answers the Following Questions:
- How do I track receivable performance?
- How do I manage my uncollectible accounts?

Key Points:
- Some of the more commonly used measures of receivable performance include:
  - Aging of Accounts Receivable - This is a distribution of outstanding accounts, arranged according to the periods they have been outstanding.
  - Days Sales Outstanding (DSO) - This measure shows on average the number of days your receivables remain outstanding.
  - Best Possible DSO (BPDSO) - This figure expresses the best possible level of receivables. The measure calculates DSO on only that portion of the open receivable base that is current.
  - Average Days Delinquent (ADD) - This figure expresses in days, the average time from the invoice due date to the paid date, or the average days invoices are past due.
  - Collection Effectiveness Index (CEI) - This percentage expresses the effectiveness of collection efforts over time. The closer to 100 percent, the more effective the collection effort. It is a measure of the quality of the collection of receivables.
- It is necessary to anticipate accounts that may prove uncollectible and then establish a reserve of profits to which such uncollectible accounts will ultimately be charged.
- Once an account is deemed to be uncollectible, it should be removed from the company's books by charging it as a write-off to bad debt expense.

Need an easy way to evaluate your customer's financial health?

CRF's FREE customer financial analysis lets you compare up to five years of customer financial information and does all the evaluating work for you.

- A spread of five periods of income statement and relevant ratios
- Five periods of balance sheet data and ratios
- Comparative operating cycles
- DuPont Ratio Analysis
- Comparative sources and uses statements
- Comparative Altman Z-Scores to anticipate the probability of business failure
- And a comprehensive summary of significant, analytical data and ratios to help you examine your customer's condition.

Visit www.crfonline.org and look for the FREE Customer Financial Statement Analysis

CONCLUSION

The receivables portfolio is generally the largest asset found on the books of businesses throughout the country. Business managers must recognize the importance of their organizations investment in receivables and the impact that efficient receivables management can have on business operations. Effective practices to manage this key asset should be put in place early on in a business that routinely extends open lines of credit to it's customers.

When establishing the receivables management process, objectives should be set that compliment the philosophy of the organization. Written policy should be devised that addresses operational procedure in the management of the organization's receivables. The policy should spell out details relating to information gathering, credit decisioning, collection process and methods to be adopted to monitor receivable performance.

All too often, business owners are not sure of what the receivables management function can do for the firm. The individual who assumes responsibility for this function must be qualified in matters related to credit and receivables management. In addition, this individual should be aware of other facets of company operations, be prepared to seek cooperation with the sales function of the organization, as well as devising procedures for achieving established goals for corporate growth. They need to be cognizant of modern methods of control and communication and continually look for the most efficient means available to attain the organization's goals and objectives. This individual should frequently review the organization and its procedures and be prepared to alter processes in an effort to create efficiency in the order to cash process. Characteristically, they should possess the ability to motivate others to do their best, a requisite for any successful manager.

Record keeping related to the receivable portfolio is imperative. A separate file, be it paper or electronic, should be set up for each customer. The individual files should contain all information related to the customers to whom you are extending open lines of credit. The file should contain billing information, contact information, credit reports on the customer, and credit and collection history related to that business. A systematic approach to assuring that the information in the credit file is kept current should be established.

Arriving at a proper and timely credit decision is difficult at best. Many factors must be taken into consideration in a relatively short span of time. Tangible factors must be evaluated, such as the customer's financial condition, credit rating and payment record. Intangible factors include the depth of management skill and your desire to maximize profits,

A key component to the credit decision-making process is the financial analysis of a potential customer's financial condition. Such an analysis involves an examination of the balance sheet, operating statement, statement of cash flows, supporting schedules, and consideration of economic conditions generally as well as in the customer's industry.

An Excel based Financial Analysis Model, that provides you with an automated tool to conduct customer financial analysis, may be obtained free of charge from CRF, by requesting it online at www.crfonline.org.

It is imperative that an effective collection procedure be put in place and strictly adhered to. Unless receivables are converted to cash on schedule, some of the company's assets are unproductively tied up. This situation causes a slow down in payments to your suppliers and forces you to seek funding through additional bank borrowings or delay production of goods due to lack of adequate cash flow. Each of these scenarios is undesirable and can have a significant impact on your firm's profitability.

Methods should be put in place specifically designed to evaluate performance of the receivable portfolio on an ongoing basis. The measures employed should be applied consistently and set up to compare receivable performance to prior periods within the organization as well as industry standards. The Credit Research Foundation has tracked standards by industry on a quarterly basis for the past 40 years through the National Summary of Domestic Trade Receivables. To gain access to this information on an ongoing basis you may contact the foundation and request to participate in the survey.

With an effective policy in place, appropriate measures of receivable performance and the proper management of the receivable function, your company can look forward to an efficient investment of its assets in accounts receivable. You will be able to anticipate the timely turnover of cash, smooth the operation of the order to cash process, enhance sales and maximize the return on your receivables portfolio.

Appendix A

Developing a Credit Strategy

A Structured Approach
You are now ready to begin designing your plan by using the following four-step process:
1. Picture your present organization.
2. Picture your organization at a future point in time.
3. Select actions that prepare for the changes.
4. Place these intended actions in a narrative format.

The first three steps can be handled by completing a relatively simple matrix. (Exhibit 1) Our method will be to examine nine critical factors that comprise the make-up of any organization, recording assessments of the present state and one that is anticipated in the future. After listing this information in the appropriate matrix columns, you will be able to compare two pictures of your firm and recognize the actions that are necessary for the transition.

The following discussion of the nine critical factors should be of help in your analysis. Also, we have used Sample Company to illustrate this process (Exhibit 2) and will follow the thought process of its credit manager as she strives to develop her department's strategic plan.

(1) Size

As your company grows in size, there will be requirements for either greater manpower or improved efficiency. Conversely, if a shrinking market is anticipated, you must adjust accordingly.

Size can be judged in a variety of ways. Historically, many firms have relied on sales volume and the number of customers to provide a reasonable measurement of workload, yet there are other considerations. In some cases, where an individual customer places many small orders, it is more appropriate to base decisions on the number of invoices that are generated. In industries where it is customary to have many price corrections or allowances, one might consider using the number of deductions, which are generated in any particular plan. Finally, a factor worth considering is the number of branch locations within your own company, since this requires interfacing with a different amount of people.

In the example that we are using (Exhibit 2), the firm has chosen to rely on the first two factors. The receivables manager has spoken to the President and learned that in the next three years sales are expected to increase from $72 million to $120 million. She has also been told that the number of customers would increase by over 20%, so these estimates are listed in the first two columns. The manager knows that this will require additional credit personnel, so she approximates an appropriate staff size and places this in the final column.

Note: You may now wish to complete this first line of information for your own firm and then follow along in a step process. You may prefer, however, to finish all nine sections and then begin your own analysis.

2) Products

The type of items that are sold, whether they are goods or services, will have a major impact on your department. For example, if your firm markets large, expensive equipment, the credit department may find itself dealing in secured transactions. Smaller items that are sold in high volume may result in a need to handle quantity discounts. Perishable products will require a quick collection of receivables, while complex machinery could lead to long range financing or leasing arrangements.

When considering a strategic plan, you must be alert to a change in product mix. If your firm will be marketing new items or differing lines of the same product, there will probably be an impact on your department. While creating new challenges, this can be seen as an opportunity for specialization within your area.

In our example, Sample Company intends to broaden their product line. Instead of simply selling standard widgets as they do today, they plan to develop lines of deluxe and multi-use widgets within the next three years. The credit manager has listed these changes in the first two blank columns, and she has drawn an obvious conclusion.

Since they will no longer deal with a homogeneous product, it is likely that different pricing structures will come into play. Realizing this, she concludes that a system will need to be developed which can monitor price deductions, and this is listed in the "Action Required" column.

3) Location

This refers to your firm's physical location and the areas in which it markets. These geographical factors can raise many long-term questions. How will you deal with people from different cultures? Will you need to change your hours to cover various time zones? As distances grow, will you have enough time for customer visits and new travel requirements?

Some credit departments have tried to address such problems by decentralizing operations. While there are apparent advantages to this approach, one should be aware of inherent disadvantages. Among them is a lack of backup for personnel, the difficulty in handling national accounts, economies of scale with regard to centralized credit sources and systems, and a loss of functional expertise, which is associated with a centralized operation. While we are not presenting a complete argument for either approach, you should be aware that this is one of the more complex issues that can be addressed.

In our example, Sample Company had previously operated and marketed in a region around a single city, Springfield. The organization plans to expand by opening two branch offices for sales, and they are even considering exporting widgets to Mexico. After listing this information, the credit manager has decided that this limited expansion does not warrant a decentralized approach. On the other hand, she realizes that additional travel may be necessary and is considering the cost-effective approach of obtaining a company car. She also knows that she will need to become more familiar with export credit procedures, and that it could be advantageous to eventually hire a bilingual collector.

This last point illustrates an important advantage to our process. Over the next few years, the credit manager may have to hire several people because of attrition or expansion. By realizing that there will be an eventual need for a bilingual collector, she can be on the lookout for such an individual during her normal hiring procedures. It will not be necessary to wait until the firm enters the Mexican market and encounters uncollectible receivables; instead, a person with such talents can be hired well before that critical stage. By planning strategically, one avoids managing by crisis.

4) Competitiveness

This factor is a primary determinant of whether your credit policy will be liberal or conservative. The strength of your position, relative to your competitors, governs how your department can respond to customers and sales opportunities.

In our example, the company is planning to expand into new markets. Leaving their established area where they enjoy a healthy 60% market share, they will be moving into other cities where they will be relatively small players. Looking at these facts, the credit manager has decided on two courses of action. First, she recognizes the necessity of learning about these new areas of opportunity so she will seek out trade associations in these cities. Second, she realizes that this lower market share will most likely require a more liberal approach to credit. As a result, she will need to work with the senior people in the organization to define an acceptable level of risk.

5) Internal Restructuring

There are very few modern corporations that have not undergone some form of restructuring in recent years. This should continue, for as Heraclitus reminded us many centuries ago, "there is nothing permanent except change". One function of a strategic plan then, is to anticipate the internal structure of your organization in the future: the relationship between departments, their functions, the roles of individuals and the people themselves. Will departments be phased out or engulfed by others? Who will control whom?

In our example, the expansion to three product lines will result in changes. After consulting with senior management, the credit manager has learned that the firm will most likely create two new sales manager positions to market the new lines. Moreover, the company is considering handling each line as a separate profit center.

After recording these anticipated changes, the manager considers how the credit department can best perform within this new environment. Obviously, there will be a need for receivable reports to be generated for each sales manager. Furthermore, anticipating a more aggressive sales posture among these new leaders, it will be necessary to provide them with incentives to control bad debt losses. The manager feels that charges against their individual Profit and Loss Statements may accomplish this aim, so her goal becomes one of developing reports and chargeback mechanisms for each sales manager. Finally, to assist them with their special needs, it appears that credit responsibilities could be structured along product lines so that sales personnel could have one-to-one relationships with their credit counterparts. All of these thoughts are summarized in the final column.

6) Economic Trends

Predicting the economic future is rarely easy, and even experts will frequently disagree. It is said that President Truman once asked the Treasury to send him a one armed economist so he would not have to hear the words, "On the other hand."

Still, economic projections are possible and useful. As tariff agreements are reached, one can decide whether this will open new markets for a firm or result in losses to lower priced foreign competition. As new tax laws or environmental rules come into being, one can calculate the effect on an organization's profitability. As the Federal Reserve gives signs of future activity, one can estimate the company's future cost of capital. Generally, your company's treasurer will have an estimate of future economic trends, and you can base your own thoughts on those assumptions.

In our Sample Company, the single projection relates to interest rates. The company is expecting to see an increase in the prime rate during the next three years, and the credit manager has adjusted her thinking accordingly. Historically, such an increase results in a greater attention to days sales outstanding. It is noteworthy that during the late 1940's, when interest rates were in low single figures, a credit manager's main responsibility was to eliminate bad debts; in the 1970's, when interest rates exceeded 15%, the role had changed to one whose primary concern was cash flow. Knowing all of this, our credit manager decides to prepare a plan, which will institute late charges.

7) Culture of the Organization

All institutions have a basic style or culture, often reflecting the temperament and leadership of senior managers. These can range from a strict environment where orders are given and obeyed to one where decisions are arrived at by consensus. While there are advantages and drawbacks to both methods, it is important that each department follows the general approach of the organization as a whole.

Sample Company had developed in a very structured atmosphere. There had been a strict chain of command for each department, and all major actions were initiated from the top managers. Now, as the firm anticipates a high rate of growth, the President feels that it will be impossible to micromanage the firm and has expressed his desire to empower the employees to make most daily decisions. Knowing that this will be a change in culture, the credit manager sees a need for two courses of action. First, her staff will require greater technical training so they can truly make decisions. Second, it will be necessary to establish a department vision, so that the empowered individuals will understand the directions they are to take in the future.

8) Systems

While computers began as a tool that would assist workers in their performance, their role has now expanded (for better or worse) to one that determines the working practices of its users. With this in mind, any strategic plan should consider the technology, which will be used in future years.

Sample Company has relied on a variety of personal computers and business packages. After speaking with technical support personnel, our credit manager has learned that the long-range goal is to integrate most departments into one system. While no real work has been done in the area yet, a number of departments such as accounting, purchasing, and sales have seen the benefit of such an approach.

The credit manager, after listing these factors in the first two blank columns of the systems line of the matrix (Exhibit 2), considers possible actions. Not wanting to leave the selection of a credit system to others, she decides to preempt the rest of the organization by making this her own department's strategic goal. She will explore various credit systems and determine the most appropriate ones that will also be compatible with future accounting and order entry processes. In this particular strategic area, the credit department will assume a leadership role.

Furthermore, as she considers the concept of an integrated system, she sees an additional opportunity for helping the organization. Remembering that pricing deductions are expected to become a greater concern for the credit area, she realizes that greater efficiency could be achieved by allowing her to absorb the billing function. While this will need to be discussed with those who presently have this responsibility, she adds this to her action plan on the matrix.

9) Legal Requirements

Obviously, any organization should behave ethically and legally. As departments change, however, it is easy to forget to review new activities to assure such compliance. This is especially true when markets are expanded into new locales that have different ordinances and regulations. Additionally, laws themselves change.

If nothing else, your strategic plan should include a general study of procedures from a legal perspective. New personnel should be trained in ethical standards and legal requirements of antitrust issues.

As we look at Sample Company, we see that they will be selling in different states and in larger amounts. Understanding that security matters can differ, the credit manager plans to review UCC procedures in these areas. She determines that this will best be accomplished with the advice of counsel, so establishing a relationship with a corporate attorney who is versed in credit matters will become a strategic goal. Finally, she will need to consider the late charges that will be implemented so they do not violate state usury laws.

The Final Steps

Once you complete the matrix for your own firm, the key elements of your strategic plan will appear in the final column. It is now time to read these action items as a whole. You may find that several comments complement each other, and they can be combined into one succinct comment. On the other hand, if you find elements that are mutually exclusive, it will be necessary to make choices. There is no sense in having a plan that cannot be implemented.

Two more points deserve emphasis

First, while we have presented a method of forming a plan that will respond to your organization's needs, it is quite possible that you will have other ideas to increase efficiency. Perhaps they will involve reduced costs or assuming new roles. These ideas can certainly be included in your plan, as long as they coincide with the organizational goals.

Second, as a team player, you will want to consult with any other departments that your plan will impact. If you feel it is beneficial for your group to absorb another area's function, it is appropriate to discuss the matter with your fellow managers. Their input will be meaningful, and if there are disagreements, your strategic plan can leave room for further study of these issues.

The final step is to place these ideas in a narrative form. While it does not have to follow the order in which the items were listed on your matrix, it should include the essential ideas. An example for Sample Company appears in Exhibit 3, and you will note that the manager has provided some reasoning behind the changes.

Exhibit 1
Sample Company Corporate Picture

ATTRIBUTE	PRESENT	IN ___ YEARS	ACTION REQUIRED TO PREPARE
Size			
Products			
Location			
Competitiveness			
Internal Restructuring			
Economic Trends			
Culture of Organization			
Systems			
Legal Requirements			

74

Exhibit 2
Sample Company Corporate Picture

ATTRIBUTE	PRESENT	IN 3 YEARS	ACTION REQUIRED TO PREPARE
Size	Sales $72 million 2700 accounts	Sales $120 million 3300 accounts	Increase credit staff from three to five
Products	Widgets (100%)	Widgets (70%) Del. Widgets (20%) Multiuse Widget (10%)	Develop system to monitor pricing deductions
Location	Springfield	Springfield, two sales branches, limited export	More travel. Company car. Learn export by taking course and develop procedures with bank. Hire bilingual collector.
Competitiveness	60% local market share	Branch locations will have less than 20% share	Join local trade associations in neighboring cities. Define levels of acceptable risk with Sr. Mgt.
Internal Restructuring	One sales mgr. with no P&L responsibility	Three Sales Mgrs. With P&L responsibility	Develop statistical reports and train administrator. Develop incentives and charges toward P&L's. Credit assignments by product.
Economic Trends	Prime rate 8%	Prime rate 11%	Greater concentration on cash flow as opposed to bad debt.
Culture of Organization	Structured. Top down decisions	Moving towards empowerment of staff	Increased credit training Establish department vision
Systems	Individual PC packages	Integrated Department programs	Explore credit systems that are compatible with accounting and order entry systems. Absorb billing part of order entry process
Legal Requirements	Presently in compliance with state laws	Selling in different states. Securing new sales	Develop UCC procedures in different states. Review late charge rates. Establish relationship with corporate attorney

75

SAMPLE COMPANY
3 Year Strategic Plan
Credit Department   *start year – end year*

In the following three years, the credit department plans to improve efficiency and make significant contributions to our corporate growth. To do this, we will implement programs and approaches that are summarized below.

Human Resources and Training

With an appreciation for the potential growth in sales revenue, customers and selling locations, we anticipate a need to gradually increase our credit staff by 2 exempt persons. An effort will be made to acquire an individual with bilingual skills so that we will be prepared for an eventual entry into the Mexican market.

Additionally, we will increase our training of credit personnel. This will be done with correspondence courses and seminars, and it may be supplemented by courses at our local university. It is our intention to establish a vision so that every credit department member will understand our corporate goals and be able to act with a high degree of independence.

In conjunction with our bank and attorney, we will develop greater expertise in the area of export credit and secured financing.

Procedures

Because of the implementation of new product lines, we expect to encounter an increase in price disputes. We will purchase a system that specializes in monitoring deductions and establish procedures for prompt resolution. We will also consider ways for the credit department to assume or improve the invoicing function.

We will help our management determine acceptable credit risks in our new markets.

To coincide with a projected sales realignment, we intend to establish credit reports, goals and incentives for each sales division. If expansion meets the projected levels, our credit department assignments will be delegated along product lines.

A system of late charges will be designed and implemented. This will be coordinated with our corporate attorney so that we remain in full compliance with lending laws.

Travel will be dramatically increased as we extend service to branch locations. We will find cost-effective ways to handle this increased service, recognizing that this may include the use of a company vehicle.

Capital Projects

We will explore available credit systems, and find ones that offer compatibility with projected accounting and order entry systems. The collection, cash application and credit referral areas will be included in any new system to meet our projected needs.

Appendix B

Developing Your Credit Policy

In order to write a policy, there are at least six questions that you and your company must answer:

- o What is our mission?
- o What are our goals?
- o Who has specific credit responsibilities?
- o How is credit evaluated?
- o How is collection handled?
- o What are our terms of sale?

Additionally, other areas you may wish to include concern your company's views on reporting, ethics, quality, training, deductions and credit interchange with other professionals.

You will now begin building a credit policy. In the following pages, you will look at each of the above questions individually. Several potential answers will be offered for each question, and you should choose one that best fits your own company. Keep in mind that there is no right or wrong answer, but the one you choose should reflect what is best for your own firm. While this is a credit policy, you should remember that you will need support from your management as well as marketing personnel. The policy needs to be advantageous to all, so it would be appropriate to consult with others when you choose answers.

Once the questions are answered, they can be put together in the format of a policy. A sample is shown in Exhibit 1. A worksheet is also available at the end of this paper for you to record and consolidate answers for your own firm.

Question 1. What is our mission?
The most important part of a policy is defining your mission. Some firms choose to call this a vision or a purpose, and it must coincide with the firm's overall direction. For example, a mission might be worded as follows:

The credit function is responsible for maintaining a high quality of accounts receivable while selling to all customers that represent prudent credit risks. Flexible mechanisms will be provided to protect the substantial receivable investment.

A company, however, that is striving to gain market share may wish to have a far more liberal credit policy. Its statement might read as follows:

It is our policy to provide credit to all potential applicants, regardless of payment experience. The credit manager will attempt to screen out customers that will result in obvious bad debts. We will attempt to build relationships with all other customers and affect collection without jeopardizing a sales relationship.

A firm that has a strong market position and is primarily concerned about its own cash flow would take a far more conservative approach toward its mission:

The credit manager is responsible for collecting our investment in accounts receivable. It is our responsibility to take no unwarranted risk, and to see that payments are made within terms. We will advise our Sales Department of customers that are risk situations and make efforts to limit our credit exposure in these areas.

These three examples represent quite different directions for a credit policy. In our sample policy (Appendix 1), the firm chose the first paragraph.

You should now choose one that best fits your company or write one of your own. Enter this on your worksheet as the first paragraph of your policy.

Question 2. What are our Goals?

You can take at least two approaches here.

First, one can write a specific set of numerical goals as follows:

Our goals are to limit bad debts to _____% of sales, Days Sales Outstanding to _____ days, and receivables aging to no more than _____% beyond 60 days. We will visit _____ customers during the next year, limit our outstanding deductions to no more than _____, and review all credit limits of over $_____. We will also cut credit department costs by $_____.

These goals must be arrived at in conjunction with your management. The Credit Research Foundation also provides many industry benchmarks that can help to arrive at reasonable goals for your firm.

A second approach is to write a generic statement on the subject:

The credit manager strives to meet goals established by senior management, which relate to bad debts, receivables aging, and Days Sales Outstanding.

This approach may be advantageous since goals frequently change. Thus, the credit policy does not require constant revision. It is important to note, however, that this should not be treated as a mechanism to ignore goal setting. Instead, written goals should be established in a separate memorandum so the entire organization understands its aims.

Our sample policy used the first approach. Now, write your policy's goal statement on your worksheet.

Question 3. Who has Specific Credit Responsibilities?

This may be the most important part of your policy statement. If properly defined, it establishes the role and authority of each individual who relates to credit. Duplication of effort is avoided and inter-company squabbling is eliminated.

An example of one policy, in which the credit manager has ultimate authority, is as follows:

The credit manager reports to the office of Treasurer. It includes all functions relating to the extension of credit, collections and cash application. The Credit Manager establishes all credit limits, has final authority to release or hold all orders when credit problems exist, decides when credit privileges should be revoked, and decides when formal credit activity should be initiated.

A more typical approach, however, recognizes a team concept within the organization. There is nothing wrong with sharing responsibility and authority as long as it is properly defined within the policy.

For example:

The credit manager reports to the office of Controller. The credit manager may establish limits of up to $_____, and the manager may delegate up to $_____ of authority to other credit personnel. The Controller of above must approve higher limits.

In the event an order is being held because of credit problems, the Sales Manager may override the decision for a single order. For further orders, the Sales Manager must review the situation with the credit manager and controller. If a consensus cannot be reached, the situation will be referred to the President for a decision.

Notice that this latter policy places some limitations on the credit manager. This should not be viewed as a loss of power. It is merely a way of providing a well-defined mechanism to achieve input from another portion of the organization. It permits the credit manager and sales manager to "agree to disagree" while still maintaining a pleasant business relationship.

Similarly, in the following example a firm has chosen to define the treatment of serious delinquency as a team approach:

When normal collection activity is exhausted, the credit manager may recommend the use of a collection agency or attorney. The Controller and sales manager will initial such requests.

You should now write one or two paragraphs that define the credit authority and responsibility within your organization, and this should be listed on your worksheet.

Question 4. How is Credit Evaluated?
Depending on the size and complexity of your organization, this section may involve a varying degree of detail. A general statement for a larger organization might be as follows:

The credit manager establishes limits for all active customers. Such limits may be based on D&B or Experian ratings, NACM reports, credit references, financial statements, security or other information obtained directly from the applicants. All decisions are judgmental with no utilization of scoring techniques.

The credit manager reviews larger limits on a periodic basis. All limits are subject to revision, based on changing levels of credit worthiness. The credit manager receives referrals of all orders that would place an account over its limit, and credit personnel may release additional orders if higher credit is justified.

You will notice that this type of statement does not provide day-to-day instructions. This company might want to develop a procedure to meet this function. An example is shown in Exhibit 2.

A different approach would be to list some details in the policy itself. This might lend itself to a smaller organization where orders are for a lower dollar volume. For example:

The sales representative will obtain a credit application from each customer. This will contain a bank reference and three trade references.

After calling references, the credit manager will determine if a customer has demonstrated the ability to pay bills in a prompt manner. If so, a credit limit will be assigned. This credit limit should not exceed the highest *extension reported by references. If a higher amount is necessary, the credit department will order a report from NACM, D&B or Experian to review further experience. Such a report will always be obtained for limits over $_____.*

For limits in excess of $_____, a financial statement will also be obtained.

Limits will periodically be reviewed. If trade experience with our company slows beyond ___ days, the limit will be revoked.

Our discussion here is obviously limited. Books have been written on this subject. What is important is to establish a consistent procedure so all potential customers are treated equally.

After considering your firm's approach to the evaluation of credit, enter comments on your worksheet.

Question 5. How is Collection Handled?
This question is at the heart of any credit policy. How you answer it will determine the major activities you perform.

Again, you may wish to rely on a general statement such as:

The collector is responsible for performing collection activity. Form letters and/or statements may be supplemented with telephone collection calls. Sales personnel will be advised of particular problems. In some cases, credit personnel will visit customers. If appropriate payment arrangements cannot be made, the credit manager may withhold further shipments.

The credit manager determines if an account is not collectable by the above means. Uncollectible accounts usually include bankruptcies, assignments to creditors, and customers that do not respond to our normal collection activities. In such cases, the accounts will be referred to collection agencies or attorneys.

An alternative company might rely solely on telephone contacts. Their policy would read:

All customers will be called when they are ___ days past due. At least three calls will be initiated. If no payments are received, the sales representative will be asked to contact the customer. If there is still no response, the Controller of our firm will decide if an account should be sent to our attorney.

Or a different approach may leave collection responsibility with the sales force:

The credit manager monitors all collection for the company. The credit manager provides sales representatives with a weekly list of customers who are _____ days past due. The sales representative makes customer contacts and advises of results. If delinquency still exists after an additional ___ days, orders are withheld.

The credit manager will then supplement these calls with final collection letters or statements. If payments are still not received after an additional _____ days, the credit manager will determine if referral to an agency is warranted.

In the case of bankruptcies, the credit manager files a proof of claim. The credit manager represents our company with creditor committees and coordinates with attorneys.

After thinking about how your collection function should work, describe it on your worksheet.

Question 6. What Are Our Terms of Sale?
It is important to have no confusion about when bills are due. For some businesses, this is not a difficult problem. They have a homogeneous product line with consistent set of terms. Thus, their policy may be relatively simple:

Terms of sale have been established by management as _____, and all credit worthy customers are expected to pay within this period.

For other companies, however, the problem may be more complex and critical. Some companies have many product lines with varying sets of terms. Other firms offer special seasonal dating. Finally, others may react to competitive practices and grant individual customers special arrangements.

These firms may choose to address the issue within their policy or with individual procedures. An example of such a policy would be as follows:

83

The standard terms of sale available for satisfactory credit risks are:

Product: Terms:

_____   _____
_____   _____
_____   _____
_____   _____

Any exceptions must be based on competitive practices and generate a satisfactory return on investment. They are to be requested by the marketing manager, reviewed for credit worthiness by the credit manager, and approved in writing by the President.

This firm might then rely on a more specific Procedure, an example of which is shown in Exhibit 3.

Now enter your own company's policy on your worksheet.

Other Factors Worth Mentioning

You now have written the basic portion of your credit policy. For many firms, this will be sufficient. Yet American industry is complex and there will probably be items that you wish to add. This could include comments on ethics, legality, quality, industry-specific programs, reporting, personnel, credit interchange and professional organizations, systems, payment deductions, returned checks, collection mechanisms, international trade, and record retention. There are undoubtedly items that belong on this list that we have not anticipated.

You will note that our sample company (Exhibit 1) has included some of these issues in a final section called Receivable Maintenance and Service. While each firm requires a different approach, we certainly recommend a statement that reinforces ethical behavior and credit professionalism.

Finally, we must remember that a policy is not a static document. It should be reviewed periodically to reflect changing circumstances. One might even consider making this part of the document itself by adding this final sentence:

This Policy will be reviewed on an annual basis.

Policy Conclusion

We began by mentioning the negative connotations of the term "Policy". Hopefully, as you have considered what will go into your own document, the positive aspects have become apparent. You should now take what you have written down, read it as a whole, and make sure it reflects what is best for your organization. This will be your credit policy.

We have resisted the temptation to take a dogmatic approach and write something for all firms. Instead, we have provided a framework for the individual credit managers to work with in a creative manner. This approach should contribute to your company's well being, your own personal satisfaction, and how our credit profession is regarded.

Exhibit 1
Sample Company's Credit Policy

Mission:
The credit manager is responsible for maintaining a high quality of accounts receivable while selling to all customers that represent prudent credit risks. We will provide flexible mechanisms to protect our substantial receivable investment.

Goals:
Our goals are to limit bad debts to ___% of sales, Days Sales Outstanding to ___ days, and receivables ageing to no more than ___% beyond 60 days. We will visit customers whenever necessary and strive to resolve all deductions within 90 days.

Organizational Responsibilities:
The credit manager reports to the office of Treasurer. Functions include the application of payments, establishing credit limits, and monitoring collection of receivables.

The credit manager establishes limits of up to $_____ and may delegate a portion of this to other department members. Higher limits are approved by the Treasurer or above. If credit privileges are withdrawn from a customer, it is our policy to consult with sales and marketing personnel in the decision process. If a consensus cannot be reached, the situation is referred to the President.

When accounts cannot be collected with normal means, the credit manager recommends the use of a collection agency or attorney. The Treasurer and sales manager approve such requests.

Credit Evaluation:
The credit manager establishes limits for all active customers. Such limits are based on trade information and financial statements when necessary. (See Exhibit 2 for a Procedure).

The department reviews larger limits on a periodic basis. All limits are subject to revision, based on changing levels of credit worthiness. Individual orders are referred to the credit manager when an account is over its limit or 15 days past due, and an effort is made to resolve such problems. If satisfactory arrangements cannot be made, the order is withheld.

Collection:
We strive to have a consistent and courteous approach to collection. All customers are called when they are ____ days past due. If no payments

are received after three calls, the sales representative is asked to contact the customer. If there is still no response, the account is considered for legal action.

In the case of bankruptcies, the credit manager files proofs of claim. The department represents our company with creditor committees and coordinates activities with attorneys.

Terms of Sale:
Terms have been established as Net ___ days. All credit worthy customers are expected to pay within this period. Any exceptions must be based on competitive practices in accordance with established procedures. (See Exhibit 3 for an example.)

Receivables Maintenance and Service:
The credit manager initiates the handling of all customer deductions promptly to assure quality receivables. Customer inquiries always receive immediate attention.

We are dedicated to behaving in a moral and legal manner.

This policy will be reviewed on an annual basis.

Policy Approvals:

_____   _____
Credit Manager   Treasurer

_____   _____
Marketing Manager   President

Exhibit 2
Sample Company

Procedure #1	**Credit Evaluation**	Effective Date: x/x/xx	Revised: x/x/xx

Purpose:

This procedure defines Sample Company's approach to evaluating new customers.

Details:

1. For any new customer, the appropriate sales representative will obtain a credit application. This will include a minimum of three trade references and telephone numbers, a bank, and the names of the principals. The sales representative will estimate the amount of credit that will be needed to service the customer within normal terms of sale. If the required limit is above $xxx,xxx, a financial statement will also be obtained.

2. The credit manager will check the D&B rating and may automatically establish limits according to the following matrix:

5A1 to 5A2	$x,xxx,xxx
4A1 to 4A2	$x,xxx,xxx
3A1 to 3A2	$x,xxx,xxx
2A1 to 2A2	$ xxx,xxx

   All other ratings will prompt an investigation by the credit manager

3. For limits under $xxx,xxx, three trade references will be called. The credit manager will consider if the customer has demonstrated an ability and willingness to pay at the required level, and a judgmental decision will be reached. If enough information is not available, additional sources such as NACM trade reports will be ordered.

4. For limits that are requested in excess of $xxx,xxx, the credit manager will always obtain a trade report from D&B, Experian, or NACM. In the absence of derogatory information such as judgments or liens, an appropriate limit will then be established.

5. For any higher limit in excess of $xxx,xxx, a financial statement will be reviewed. Considerations will include liquidity and debt capacity. In general, we will require positive working capital, a debt/equity ratio of no more than 3:1, and our limit will not exceed 25% of the applicants net worth unless approved by senior management.

6. Before rejecting any customer whose potential volume exceeds $x,xxx,xxx annually, the application will be forwarded to the controller for review.

7. If necessary, the credit department may rely on guarantees or Letters of Credit to complete sales.

8. If open terms cannot be justified, the customer will always be given the opportunity to purchase on a cash basis.

9. For all accounts with limits in excess of $xxx,xxx, a new credit report will be obtained annually.

Exhibit 3
Sample Company

Procedure #2	Competitive Arrangements Revised: x/x/xx	Effective Date: x/x/xx

Purpose:

Normal terms offered by Sample Company are Net xx days. At times, we may find that a customer is offered a longer set of terms by competition. This procedure outlines steps that we will take when a customer requests that we be competitive in this area.

Details:

1. The sales representative will confirm that a competitor is truly offering different terms of sale. This will be accomplished by actually seeing an invoice or letter offering these arrangements. We will not initiate non-standard terms, but we will consider meeting competitive practices.

2. The sales representative will complete a memorandum, addressed to the sales manager, which includes the following:

   a. What arrangements specific competitors are offering?

   b. What are our annual sales?

   c. What is our anticipated gross profit?

   d. How much additional receivables will be outstanding if we offer this competitive arrangement?

   e. Based on a cost of capital of x%, what will be the cost of carrying these receivables?

   f. For how long would we be expected to continue this arrangement?

3. The sales manager will review the request and determine if marketing factors justify granting this request. If so, the memorandum will be initialed with a recommendation for approval and forwarded to the Credit Manager.

4. The credit manager will review the situation from a standpoint of additional risk. If in agreement, the request will be approved and

forwarded to the President for final approval. Otherwise, it will be returned to the marketing manager with comments that detail the credit difficulties.

5. The President will make a final judgment. If the President approves the arrangement, the sales representative will be instructed to notify the customer.

6. The credit manager will take steps to adjust agings and delinquency letters to reflect new arrangements. The department will monitor the account to be sure that the special arrangement is followed.

Credit Policy Worksheet

Mission:

_____

_____

_____

_____

Goals:

_____

_____

_____

_____

Organizational Responsibilities:

_____

_____

_____

Credit Evaluation:

_____

_____

_____

_____

Collection:

_____

_____

_____

_____

Terms of Sale:

_____

_____

_____

_____

Credit Policy Worksheet
(Continued)

Receivable Maintenance and Service:

_____
_____
_____
_____

Approvals:

_____
_____
_____
_____

Appendix C

Developing a Job Description:

The job description should be drafted based on the specifications of the job analysis. It should indicate what, why, where, and how a job is to be done.

The Main Features Of The Job Description Are:

- Identification of the job title, department and reporting relationships (when applicable, include the date of the last job analysis, a job number, the present number of employees in that position and the pay scale).
- A description of the general responsibilities and components.
- Specific duties, tasks and responsibilities (including materials or machinery used, working conditions, or special instruments required).
- Identification of performance-related job tasks and critical skills. These skills should be broken down by the knowledge needed to perform the job function, the proficiency level required in each skill area (basic, intermediate, or advanced), and the level of responsibility for each task.
- Specific education and experience required.
- Any additional requirements for the job (such as travel requirements).

Use of Action Verbs in Job Descriptions:

When writing a job description, it is important to use action verbs to describe the tasks and to have duties grouped together that have a logical flow. The following guide could be used when preparing the "specific duties" area of the job description:

- Begin with the action verb
- State what does it apply to
- State how the information is obtained
- State how, why and how often is it done.

Example:

Action verb	What it applies to	How the information is obtained	How, why and how often
Analyzes	Requests for credit	Received from customers and credit information sources	By evaluating financial statements, credit reports, and reference information, to establish a workable credit line every six months.

When job analysis and job description systems are in place, staffing requirements and, future staffing plans are possible. The recruitment process is clear because the requirements and qualifications of the position are defined. The salary range has already been determined, eliminating wasted time of interviewing candidates who have salary expectations and needs beyond your range. The most qualified candidate may then be selected. The candidate has a clear knowledge of the job requirements, to whom they report and how it relates to the other functions of an organization. Many times, the career path is also defined and career planning by the employee becomes possible, making the job opening more desirable and recruitment of qualified candidates an easier process.

When a job analysis and job description are done for a position that is already filled but no documentation exists, the analysis and description may be used to assess any training needs and assist in establishing training programs. Performance appraisals, based on the requirements of a job analysis and job description, have more validity because the parameters of the tasks and skills required to do the tasks have already been defined. A clear benchmark exists. Areas that need improvement may be identified and the training process may begin. The employee also has a clear view of what is expected, how they are doing, and where improvement is needed. This knowledge empowers an employee to determine a realistic career path.

The importance of the job analysis and job description extends beyond the selection process. By providing a definition of the component parts of a job, boundaries are set and confusion is limited concerning what is supposed to be done and who is responsible. Important aspects of the job analysis and job description include:

- Defining component parts of a job to eliminate confusion
- Providing legal protection to the employer with documentation
- Assisting in developing and selecting training programs
- Determining an equitable pay range for the position

- Improving the accuracy of the performance appraisal for the specific position

One way to ensure compliance with the EEOC is to have a clear plan and backup to address the criteria employers' use in making employment related decisions in the initial selection process, promotions, layoffs and termination actions by employers. The job analysis, and job description (especially when used with performance appraisals in a termination) can provide legitimate reasoning for the actions taken by a company when selecting, promoting or terminating employees.

Together, they provide a work environment that has clear descriptions of what is expected on the job and how well these expectations are being met.

Job Analysis Worksheet

1. Official Title of Position

_____

2. Classification of Position

___ Part time   ___ Seasonal
___ Full time   ___ Exempt
___ Permanent   ___ Non- Exempt
___ Temporary

3. Title of immediate supervisor

_____

4. Title of next management level

_____

5. Department or area of responsibility

_____

6. Division, Section, Unit (where applicable)

_____

7. Schedule of Hours

_____

8. The task is determined by:

What action is performed?

_____

_____

Who or what is affected?

_____

_____

What is produced?

_____

_____

What equipment is needed?

_____

What the process is?

_____

_____

What knowledge, and level (basic, intermediate, or advanced) is needed to perform the job?

_____

What specific abilities and skills are needed to perform the job?

_____

What minimum level of education and experience is required?

_____

How much time and what source of training is needed?

_____

9. If the position is a supervisory one, indicate the number and title of employees to be supervised.

_____   _____

_____   _____

_____   _____

_____   _____

10. The extent of supervision for the position being examined (e.g., assignment of work, review of work, approval of work, training, performance evaluations, hiring, promoting, firing, disciplinary actions, procedures, work flow management).

_____

_____

11. Any and all guidelines needed for completion of task.

_____

_____

12. Who will supervise this position and the extent of the required supervision (e.g., assignment of work, review of work, approval of work, training, performance evaluations, hiring, promoting, firing, disciplinary actions, procedures, work flow management)?

_____

13. Accountability: Through what processes are errors found (e.g., to whom is work handed-off) and who is responsible for the corrections?

_____

_____

14. Are unusual physical demands required in this position (e.g., heavy lifting)?

_____

15. What are the working conditions to perform the job (e.g., environment, office, warehouse, etc.)?

_____

_____

16. Is the safety of others a responsibility of this position?

_____

17. What type of interaction is there with others, how often, with whom, why?

_____

_____

18. Extent of exposure to confidential information and possible effects of breech classified information?

_____

19. Any other requirements (e.g., travel, extensive overtime, etc.)?

_____

_____

Job Description Worksheet

1. Official Title of Position and Department

_____

2. To whom does the position report?

_____

3. If a supervisory role, how many are supervised and their function (e.g., supervisory responsibility for 3 collections specialist, 2 credit analysts etc.)?

____   _____

____   _____

____   _____

____   _____

4. General objective; use action verbs such as: establish, prepare, conduct, analyze, etc. (e.g., To establish credit policies and practices and to administer all levels of credit administration.)

_____

_____

5. Specific duties (use answers from question 8 of the Job Analysis Worksheet)

_____

_____

6. Education requirement for position and level of experience (e.g., BS in Business, Certified Credit Executive, plus three years experience with a proven track record for decreasing average days delinquent)

_____

7. Any additional requirements

_____

_____

8. List salary range

_____ to _____

Appendix D

Sample Credit Application:

YOUR LOGO

Sales Rep:_____Date_____

Analyst:_____

Your Company Address
Phone #
Fax#

Credit Application

CONSENT AGREEMENT

The undersigned hereby consent(s) to *(Your company name)* use of a non-business consumer credit report on the undersigned in order to further evaluate the credit worthiness of the undersigned as principal(s), proprietor(s) and/or guarantor(s) in connection with the extension of business credit as contemplated by this credit application. The undersigned hereby authorize(s) *(Your company name)* to utilize a consumer credit report on the undersigned from time to time in connection with the extension or continuation of the business credit represented by this credit application. The undersigned as [an] individual(s) hereby knowingly consent to the use of such credit report consistent with the Federal Fair Credit Reporting Act as contained in 15 U.S.C. @1681 et seq.

Authorized Signature	Title	Date
X		

COMPANY DATA

Legal Name:	Telephone:
Trade Name(s):	Fax:
Street Address:	Billing Address:

Type of Company: ☐ C Corporation ☐ Sub S Corporation ☐ LLC ☐ Partnership ☐ Proprietorship ☐ Other

Are you current on all applicable franchise taxes? ☐ Yes ☐ No. If No, please explain:

Bankruptcy ☐ No ☐ Yes   If yes, when filed?_____ ☐ Chapter 11 ☐ Chapter 7 ☐ Other

Date Started:	Dun & Bradstreet No. (DUNS No.):
Date Incorporated:	Federal Tax ID:
State of Incorporation:	Parent Company Name:

Accounts Payable Contact:	Telephone:	Fax:
	E-Mail:	
Purchasing Contact:	Telephone:	Fax:
	E-Mail:	

If items printed are for resale, attach a copy of your resale certificate (State Sales Tax Exemption certificate) with an original

PRINT REFERENCES (Current and Past)

Contact Name:	Telephone:	Fax:
Company Name:	E-Mail:	
City / State:	Your Customer No.:	
Contact Name:	Telephone:	Fax:
Company Name:	E-Mail:	
City / State:	Your Customer No.:	

TRADE REFERENCES (Current and Past)

Contact Name:	Telephone:	Fax:
Company Name:	E-Mail:	
City / State:	Your Customer No.:	
Contact Name:	Telephone:	Fax:
Company Name:	E-Mail:	
City / State:	Your Customer No.:	

Appendix D (continued)

Sample Credit Application (page 2):

YOUR LOGO

Your Company Address
Phone #
Fax#

FINANCIAL STATEMENTS

For a requested credit limit in excess of $10,000, please attach a copy of your most recent fiscal year-end financial statements, including balance sheet, income statement, and cash flow report. This information is essential to the extension of credit. Be assured that any information that you provide will be used solely to evaluate your creditworthiness.

In consideration of the extension of credit and establishment of a credit account, applicant acknowledges liability for payment of amounts due *(Your company name)* or its subsidiaries. If *(Your company name)* must take action to collect any balance owing, applicant agrees to pay all reasonable costs and expenses incurred in collection including, but not limited to, reasonable attorney's fees, court costs, and interest thereon at the then maximum legal rate. By signing this agreement, applicant acknowledges payment will be made according to quoted terms on invoice. All past due invoices are subject to interest charges of the lessor of 18% per annum or the maximum allowable legal rate. Signature also authorizes the release of credit information concerning our company that *(Your company name)* may reasonably require.

Authorized Signature	Title	Date
X		

Bank Reference

TO BE COMPLETED BY CUSTOMER

Name of Customer:	Name of Bank:
Address:	Address:
Telephone:	Telephone: Fax:
Account No.:	Account Officer:

We hereby authorize our bank, named above, to release complete credit information to *(Your company name)* via fax. This includes information on depository accounts and any borrowing relationship we may have. This authorization shall remain in effect until written notice is received from an authorized signer.

Authorized Signature(s):

X _____

X _____

X _____

Date: _____

Title: _____

Title: _____

Title: _____

PLEASE FAX COMPLETED FORM TO:

(YOUR COMPANY NAME)(YOUR FAX#)

ATTN. _____   DATE _____

About The Credit Research Foundation

Chartered in 1949, CRF is an organization emphasizing the impact and contribution of the credit function on individual businesses and the national economy. Our forums, reports, surveys and other publications provide valuable information on new technique and trends in credit and accounts receivable administration and practices, along with information technology applications to support credit, accounts receivable, and cash management functions.

The Credit Research Foundation, an independent organization formed as a non-profit corporation, has its own membership, Board of Trustees and committee structure. The only requirement for membership in the Foundation is a sincere, vested interest in the activities of business-to-business credit.

The objectives of the Foundation are:

- To encourage, foster, and promote a comprehensive understanding of credit and accounts receivable management emphasizing the importance of sound practices in both these and related areas of financial administration.

- To promote the interest of the entire credit profession and related fields in financial management.

- To develop and maintain active programs of research and education in the fields of credit, accounts receivable and financial management.

- To provide a resource for credit and customer financial service professionals contributing to advanced skills development and enhancement of the receivable portfolio management.

Other Publications from CRF

The following publications are available from the Credit Research Foundation. You may view a detailed description of each of the publications and order them on the web by clicking on *Publications* at www.crfonline.org.

1. Credit Professional's Handbook

2. Management Reports

3. CRF's 2002 Credit & Accounts Receivable ERP System Study

4. The Future of Business Credit

5. The Credit and Financial Management Review

6. Coming to Terms

7. Secured Transactions

8. Credit Deserves Credit

9. Bad Check Laws

10. Outsourcing and the Collection Function

11. The Guide for Career and Professional Development In Business Credit

12. Measures of Performance

13. Credit & A/R Compensation Study
    How to Write a Credit Policy

14. Customer Deductions: Impact on Receivables

15. The Credit Professional's Guide To Bankruptcy

16. The Credit Professional's Guide To Creditors' Committees in Chapter 11

17. Commencing An Involuntary Bankruptcy Petition: The Credit Executive's Perspective

18. The Credit Professional's Preference Manual